MW01280093

Chaplain (LTC) Milton S. Herring I (US Army Ret.)

Mobilizing
The Army Of God
In the 21st Century

Chaplain (LTC) Milton S. Herring I (US Army Ret.)

Mobilizing
The Army Of God
In the 21st Century

ARMOUR OF LIGHT
PUBLISHING
Chapel Hill, North Carolina · Charleston, South Carolina

Published in the United States of America by
Armour of Light Publishing
P.O. Box 778
Chapel Hill, North Carolina 27514

Visit us at: www.armouroflight.org

Design by Michael E. Evans

ISBN 978-0-9825476-4-9

Library of Congress Control Number: 2010911063

First Edition

All scriptures quoted from the Authorized King James Version unless otherwise noted.

10 9 8 7 6 5 4 3 2 *1*

Dedication

This book is dedicated to my beloved mother, Mary Adele Hollins Herring, who nurtured me both physically and spiritually. She believed in me and encouraged me until the Lord called her to her eternal rest.

And to the memory of my beloved sister, Maxine Legretta Noble Wilson (1945-2009), who was always one of my greatest encouragers.

Also, to my uncle/dad, Deacon John W. Wynne (1932-2010), who from my earliest recollections took me to church and was my role model for a Godly man, husband, and father. His prayers meant so much to me.

And to all the men and women, in uniform, serving our great country: Thank you for your service.

Acknowledgments

I would like to thank some key people who have helped me with the significant task of publishing this book. First of all I must acknowledge my Heavenly Father, my Lord and liberator Jesus Christ for moving by the Holy Spirit in my life and giving me the vision for this book. Secondly, without the valuable assistance of my wife, Cinda, who provided the support I needed in so many areas, this book would not have made it to print. She is truly the 'wind beneath my wings'.

I would like to thank my son Milton, Jr. and his wife Sherry, for proof reading and their timely suggestions. To all the members of Living Word Church in Torrance, Ca., and in Kuwait, for your prayers and support as I shared in sermons and teachings about the mandate God has given me. Thanks to Randy Dean and Teresa Rhynes for proof reading.

Throughout the writing of this book, I have gleaned from several awesome men and women of God; I will list a few, t it am grateful to them all. One of my spiritual fathers Bishop Keith A. Butler has been just a blessing to my wife and me. His teachings and personal life style have had a great impact on my life. Dr. Bill Winston and Dr. Myles Monroe have taught me much about the Kingdom of God.

I would like to thank Pastors Johnny and Elizabeth Enlow for the time they spent listening to and encouraging me, and their teachings on the Seven Mountains strategy and Mantle. Elders Leroy Williams and Carl Moore have pastored and mentored me throughout my journey of faith and imparted their wisdom to me, giving me the spiritual fortitude for undertaking this task. Reverend Jeff Moffett, who served with me in Kuwait in 2004-2005, and was co-teaching a Bible class with me when God gave me the vision of 'Advancing the Kingdom of God' and has been my sounding board in so many ways.

To my publisher, Michael E. Evans, his wife Gloria, and the team at Armour Of Light; thank you for helping me realize this dream.

Finally, I must acknowledge my Chaplain assistants who served with me in Kuwait, Sergeants Anthony Miltenbuger and John Barrow, and all those who served in the 'Gospel services' for your prayers and encouragement. More than you know, you helped to make this book a reality.

Table of Contents

The Beloved Community

The Calling

Chapter 1
I Got Drafted

"Ye have not chosen me, but I have chosen you, and ordained you, that ye should go and bring forth fruit, and that your fruit should remain: that whatsoever ye shall ask of the Father in my name, he may give it you."

John 15:16

My military journey began when I received a letter from Uncle Sam in 1969. I was twenty years of age, not long out of high school, and working full time for Ford Motor Company. And then --

I got drafted!

Now, to be drafted, by definition, is to be selected for some purpose. Sounds noble now, but it didn't feel that way at the time. The Vietnam War was in full swing and that letter meant I had to go. I had to go and serve my country. There was a greater purpose behind my military service, but I didn't know that at the time.

Conscription in the United States (also called compulsory military service or the draft) has been employed several times, usually during war but also during the nominal peace of the Cold War. The United States discontinued the draft in 1973 during the Nixon administration, moving to an all-volunteer military force, thus there is currently no mandatory conscription--no draft.

Because it has been almost thirty years, the draft may seem like some archaic practice of the faraway past. That distance seems to have adversely affected the perception of people in the body of Christ. It appears that Christians think their service to God and his kingdom is completely voluntary as well. I know we have free will, but make no mistake: God has never stopped calling, choosing, and commissioning men and women into the service of His kingdom.

I got drafted! And, believe it or not, you did too.

You have been selected for some purpose. God's eternal purpose may be carefully hidden within a more obvious immediate purpose, but you can be sure, God has a plan for all of us.

My draft letter came shortly after I had received the news that one of my best friends, Dwight Foster, was dead. Dwight enlisted with the promise that he would not go to Vietnam. Dwight not only went to Vietnam, he was killed in action.

I had heard that every Black man going into the Army was being sent to the front line and I was not at all interested in dying for my country. So, I went to talk with an Air Force recruiter who promised me that, rather than fighting, I would receive job training. I entered the Air Force in September, 1969 and went to do my basic training at Lackland AFB, in San Antonio, Texas.

As I was about to complete basic training, I was informed that because I was partially color blind, I was not eligible to train in my chosen field of electrical engineering and that I would be placed to "fill the needs of the Air Force." I did get assigned to work in the Civil Engineering Squadron, but as a plumbing specialist. I didn't realize then that I was also being trained to be used wherever God needed me.

At first I was not too happy about becoming a plumber, but the more I thought about it the more I became excited about the opportunity. I had met a black man in Detroit who owned his own plumbing shop and he seemed to be doing quite well. I began to imagine myself doing well, also. Soon, I had a plan. I would allow the Air force to train me and after four years I would get out and work towards starting my own plumbing company.

Upon completing my training school at Sheppard AFB, Wichita Falls, Texas in December, 1970, I reported to my first duty assignment at Mather AFB, just east of Sacramento, California. As I settled into my new surroundings for the next two years, I unpacked a booklet given to me by my pastor in Detroit, Michigan when I was leaving Detroit and the church I had served in since I was 12 or 13. I had come a long way since those beginning days.

Mobilizing The Army of God

Chapter 2

Recruiting The Youth

"America's Army" is a video game designed by the US Army. Josh White, a staff writer for the *Washington Post* reported on Friday, May 27, 2005, that the game is "an online, multi-player video game that the Army believes will lure teenagers into Army culture, hoping both to educate them about the military and to spark interest in volunteering to serve."

That's a great idea, but not an original one. Jesus told the disciples to *"Suffer the little children to come unto me, and forbid them not: for of such,"* the Lord said, *"is the kingdom of God"* (Mark 10:14). Jesus also warned his followers that he was sending them forth as, *"...sheep in the midst of wolves."* He warned them to be *"wise as serpents, and harmless as doves"* (Matthew 10:16)

One summer day, while some friends and I were playing football in the streets, someone told us about a lady who was serving cookies and punch in her basement not far away. Several of us took off running to the house.

We arrived at the back door and knocked furiously until this little lady maybe 5'5" came to the door. We asked about the punch and cookies and she smiled and said; "We don't serve until after Sunday school, which is just starting." We looked at each other, and most of the guys left. But I said to my best friend Robert Williams; "Man, come on. It couldn't hurt."

We went into the basement of that house, and Billy Taylor was teaching the class. I knew Billy. He lived just down the street. Billy was a few years older than us, and I looked up to him. During the class Billy would ask some of us to read a verse or two. I did okay with my reading, but Robert could not read some of the words, which is why I think he never came back.

After the class, just as promised, we had our fill of cookies and punch. As we were leaving, the nice lady approached us and asked, "Will you all be back next Sunday?" to which I replied, "Will you have more cookies and punch?" "Of course, we will," she said. "Then we'll be back."

Robert wouldn't join me, but I kept coming. Soon, I had my family coming too--all except my dad. We outgrew the basement and moved into a storefront building. I was baptized in that storefront. I became a Sunday school teacher and then superintendent of the Sunday school in that storefront. I even served on the trustee board at the tender age of 18 in that storefront. I learned public speaking and how to conduct a meeting during these formative years. All because a little lady was wise enough to know that little boys will do almost anything for punch and cookies. Video games hadn't been invented yet.

As I was preparing to leave the nest of the Church of the Living God C.W.F.F. (Christians Workers For Fellowship), Elder Greenhill gave me a journal which listed all of the churches in our brotherhood association. I was delighted when I found one in Sacramento, California.

20

I contacted the pastor, Evangelist Maxine Kirkland. She agreed to come to the base and pick me up for dinner at her home one Saturday. I readily accepted the invite for a home cooked meal. I was never one to turn down an invite for some home cooking. She came and picked me up and on the way to her home she drove past the church. It was a small building on a street called Lemon Hill.

The next day, I borrowed a friend's car and drove to the church. Being interested in Sunday school, I arrived at the church early. In fact, I was the first to arrive. I got out of the car and walked around the building familiarizing myself with the area.

Soon a car pulled up with two women. I introduced myself to Deloma Finch, the Sunday school superintendent, and her beautiful, single, daughter Cinda. Mrs. Finch unlocked the door and I walked in and continued my causal walk around with my hands behind my back. I was sensing in my spirit that this would be my church home for the two years I would be assigned to Mather AFB. My reflective time was interrupted when Cinda said, "So are you casing the place?" and flashed her gorgeous smile. We both laughed. That was the beginning of a relationship that would last until this day.

When Evangelist Kirkland learned of my experiences in Detroit, she quickly got me involved in the church ministry in Sacramento. I also met another pastor Elder Carl Moore, who lived in Sacramento and pastored a church in Bakersfield. I started spending time with him and even driving with him to Bakersfield sometimes.

He was very knowledgeable about the Bible and became a mentor for me. He gave me a thirst to know more about the Bible. The thoughts that I had early in my life about preaching were getting stronger and more frequent. But for now, I was focused on starting my own plumbing business.

Soon, I purchased my first car--a used 1962 Oldsmobile, white with blue interior. Since my days in Detroit, I had a passion for the Olds. By now Cinda and I were dating. She had a car and would sometimes come to the base and pick me up. Now that I had my own car, I was excited to be able to pick her up and take her home.

One day, while taking her home after church, I remember being blinded by the sun. I never saw the car stopped at a light ahead of us and I rear-ended that car. Cinda was not wearing a seat belt and she was sitting as close as possible to me.
Her face slammed into the dash board and her front teeth were knocked back into her mouth. She lay mangled in the front floor. My chest broke the steering wheel and I busted my lip on the dash board. The car was crushed. The paramedics had to pry us both from the wreckage.

Cinda's brother Gregory would tell us later that the car was totaled and it is a miracle that anybody walked away from that accident. Cinda would undergo some surgery especially extensive dental surgery, but praise the Lord she made it through.

As I reflected on that automobile accident, which could have been fatal, I began thinking seriously about what I was doing with my life. I knew that God had called me into the ministry and some day I knew I would submit, but not just yet.

Cinda and I were becoming serious about each other and we talked about our future together. I had started taking college courses at night on base and had decided rather than becoming a plumber, I would become a lawyer.

Although, I was wrestling with the Holy Spirit about yielding my life to Him, I had come to grips with one thing for sure. I had decided that I wanted Cinda Finch in my life forever. She brought so much joy into my life. She graduated from high school and enrolled into UC Davis, and shortly thereafter we were engaged. We did not plan on getting married for some time, but those plans would soon change.

My two year tour was about up and I received orders for Yokota, AFB, Japan, with a report date of September, 1971. We decided, with the blessing of her mother, to move our wedding up to August, so that Cinda could come to Japan-- as my wife.

Mobilizing The Army of God

Chapter 3
Surrender In Japan

I arrived in Japan in 1971, assigned to a RED HORSE Civil Engineering Squadron. This tour of duty in the 'Land of the Rising Sun' would prove to be a turning point in my life.

First of all, according to the Air Force Civil Engineer Support Agency and US Air Force Central, "RED HORSE (Rapid Engineer Deployable Heavy Operational Repair Squadron Engineers) squadrons provide the Air Force with a highly mobile civil engineering response force to support contingency and special operations worldwide. Units are self-sufficient 404-person mobile squadrons capable of rapid response and independent operations in remote, high-threat environments worldwide. They provide heavy repair capability and construction support when requirements exceed normal base civil engineer capabilities and where Army engineer support is not readily available.

RED HORSE units possess weapons, vehicles/equipment and vehicle maintenance, food service, emergency management, contracting, supply and medical equipment and personnel.

RED HORSE's major wartime responsibility is to provide a highly mobile, rapidly deployable, civil engineering response force that is self-sufficient to perform heavy damage repair required for recovery of critical Air Force facilities and utility systems, and aircraft launch and recovery. In addition, it accomplishes engineer support for beddown of weapon systems required to initiate and sustain operations in an austere bare base environment, including remote hostile locations, or locations in a chemical, biological, radiological, nuclear and high-yield explosives (CBRNE) prone environment.

The primary RED HORSE tasking in peacetime is to train for contingency and wartime operations. It participates regularly in Joint Chiefs of Staff and major command exercises, military operations other than war, and humanitarian civic action programs. RED HORSE performs training projects that assist base construction efforts while, at the same time, honing wartime skills. Air Force RED HORSE units possess special capabilities, such as water-well drilling, explosive demolition, aircraft arresting system installation, quarry operations, concrete mobile operations, material testing, expedient facility erection, and concrete and asphalt paving."

1. http://www.afcesa.af.mil/library/factsheets/factsheet.asp?id=8760
2. http://www.centaf.af.mil/news/story.asp?id=123168016

During this assignment God was building some infrastructure in me, too. I met another airman in the pool hall at the base recreation center. Both of us thought we were the best pool players in Japan, and that competitive catalyst was enough to spark a spirited relationship. Sergeant Robert J. V. McMillan would become a life long friend.

Sgt. McMillan was married and had a daughter named Regina. The McMillans lived off base in what we called 'Patty Homes'. 'Patty Homes' were wood framed houses, heated with kerosene. Cinda and I would live there also when she arrived. McMillan would be a great help to us in making the transition. He and his wife Katie invited us over for dinner and we learned that we all loved singing gospel music. Now, I couldn't carry a tune in a bucket, but that didn't keep us from making a joyful noise every time we got together. We also worshipped together at the base Chapel.

One night while standing in line at the base theatre we found ourselves complaining about the "dry" worship services and imagining how much a gospel choir would "liven things up." Well, this conversation led us to the point of action; we approached the base chaplain about starting a gospel choir. The chaplain was very supportive and we put the word out around the base. Before long we had a musician, a director (Mrs. Brown), and a thirty voice choir.

The Yokota Angelic Gospel Choir became very popular and attendance for the worship services increased. The chaplain invited the choir to sing at the 1972 memorial service for Dr. Martin Luther King, Jr. I was very excited about this until I found out who the speaker would be.

In case I painted too pristine a picture in the last chapter, make no mistake, the cookies and punch that drew me to Christ were not served in Mayberry, RFD. My upbringing was on the mean streets of inner-city Detroit, Michigan. I came up during a time of serious racial tension in our nation. And as a young, Black, semi-militant, I was influenced by more than just my church. The Black Panthers, The Church of the Black Madonna and the Black Muslims all had a hand in shaping my worldview.

Additionally, my grandfather, James Revis, Sr., was very much involved in the civil rights movement in Birmingham, Alabama. He was a trustee for Bethel Baptist Church, pastored by the Reverend Fred Shuttlesworth--the father of the Civil Rights movement in Birmingham. In the summer of 1962, my grandfather took me along with others on a chartered bus to Atlanta, Georgia, for a Southern Christian Leadership Conference (SCLC) meeting.

I recall sitting in a very boring meeting and afterwards being pulled around the church to the altar by my grandfather to shake hands with the person who had been leading this boring meeting. (I found out years later that it was a business meeting.) It was Dr. Martin Luther King, Jr. I will never forget placing my small hand into his massive, but very soft, hands. Since that day, whenever I hear his name, I am glad that I met Dr. Martin Luther King, Jr.

A decade later, however, I was not glad when I learned that a white chaplain would be giving the message for Dr. King. I was, in fact, very angry. I thought, "What could a white man possibly tell me about someone so special to people of color?" I almost decided not to attend, but my curiosity got the best of me.

After the choir sang, we left the choir stand to sit in the congregation. I sat as close as possible to the front with my arms defiantly folded. All I remember is that by the time the chaplain was finished, so was I. I was moved almost to tears. I was on the edge of my seat, in awe, for most of his speech. And I gladly admit, I was greatly impressed.

This white chaplain presented the life and message of Dr. King in a way that I had never heard. Unbeknownst to me, the Holy Spirit was doing heavy damage repair in me and both the message and the messenger were paving the way for me to answer the call on my life. Suddenly I knew I wanted to continue the work of Dr. Martin Luther King, Jr. And I wanted to do so as a military chaplain.

I don't remember the chaplain's name, but I do remember that after he finished his speech, I waited to talk with him and I made an appointment to meet with him. Over the course of several one-on-one sessions, he discipled me and helped me come to grips with my calling. I shared this with my wife and we prayed about it along with the McMillans. I began a quest to know God more intimately, through periods of fasting and praying. Then something incredible happened.

One day, while, driving the plumber's utility van going on a house call for a job, I stopped to pray. The van was parked when I sensed such an awesome move of the Holy Spirit that I could not stand. I fell to the floor of that van and had a personal encounter with Jesus. I heard Him say to me, *"I am the Way, the Truth and the Life."* It was there on the floor of a US Air Force utility van that I surrendered my life to the Living Lord, Jesus Christ.

My life forever changed, and I knew I would now have to explain to my wife that the lawyer she thought she was marrying would, in fact, become a minister of the gospel.

During my next session with the chaplain, I said to him, "Sir, I have decided that I want to do what you are doing. I want to become a chaplain." He explained the educational re-

quirements for becoming a chaplain and I knew that taking
college courses in the evening, as I was doing, would take
me a very long time to accomplish my new goal.

My wife and I made the decision to get out of the military so
that I could become a full-time student in order to complete
my education as soon as possible and return to the Air Force
as a chaplain.

Chapter 4
A Dream Delayed

Once the decision was made to surrender to the call of God on my life and become a full time student, the next decision was which college I would attend. As I pondered this decision, I thought about the man who had made such an impact on my life--Dr. Martin Luther King, Jr. As I read more about his life I learned that he had attended Morehouse College. Morehouse had prepared him for his destiny and I believed they could prepare me for mine, as well. It was settled. I too would apply to this famed all male institution for higher learning. I wanted to experience the mystique of Morehouse and join the ranks of the elite "Morehouse Man." You can always tell a Morehouse Man--but you can't tell him much!

We moved to Atlanta and I started the winter semester in 1974 with almost two years of transferable college credits. This enabled me to complete my Bachelor of Arts requirements in August 1976. Because I was a man on a mission I went to summer school each year and enrolled in seminary a month after graduation. I graduated from the Interdenominational Theological Center (ITC) in 1979 with a Masters of Divinity degree.

It seemed like I was on track for reaching my goal of becoming an Air Force chaplain until I discovered that not only is there an educational requirement for becoming a chaplain, but there is a also an ecclesiastical requirement.

A person must be endorsed by a recognized religious body before he is eligible to become an Air Force chaplain. The operative word being 'recognized'. Unfortunately, The Church of the Living God (C.W.F.F.) was not recognized, and had never even applied to be recognized. "No problem," I thought. I would do the leg work necessary for my church to become recognized. But, after months of working with denominational leaders to go through the process, I finally accepted the painful reality that it was not to be.

Shortly thereafter I met and began to learn from another great preacher, Reverend Rudolph Smith of Community Church of God in Atlanta, Georgia. My wife and I worshipped there while we lived in Atlanta and he took us in under watch care. That is to say, we were considered members without actually joining the church. I became one of his first associate ministers.

Rev. Smith was a graudate of Interdominational Theological Center (ITC) and very skilled in the Bible. He was also a very powerful preacher. He and his wife, Sister Edna Smith, became spiritual parents to us and Rev. Smith became one of my mentors. His son, Rev. Michael Smith and I became friends. We both attended Morehouse and ITC together. As of this writing, Rev. Michael Smith is serving as the senior pastor of Community Church of God in Atlanta, Georgia.

When Rev. Smith learned of my situation, he offered to help me, provided I would be willing to become a part of the Church of God, Anderson, Indiana. I prayed about it, but decided I would not leave my childhood church (even though many of my Bishops had said I would after completing my education).

It seemed as if my dream of becoming a military chaplain would never be realized, so in 1980 I entered an intern program for becoming an administrator for a long term health care facility. Upon completion of the internship, I was offered a job in Los Angeles, California by Mr. John A Jackson, Executive Director of The Stovall Foundation.

I had been a local pastor while I was in seminary. My first church assignment was in McKenzie, Alabama, a four hour drive, one way, from Atlanta, Ga. After one year there I was assigned to Birmingham, Ala. I served in Birmingham for two years before being asked to start a church in Atlanta, Georgia.

Counting our two children, the church had about fifteen or twenty members. Two of our members were our next door neighbors, Dexter and Barbara Easley. After a time of our witnessing to him, Dexter gave his life to the Lord. He later surrendered to the call on his life. At the time of this writing, Dr. Dexter Easley pastors New Life Christian Fellowship in Goose Creek, South Carolina. We remain friends until this day.

The presiding bishop of The Church of the Living God, Bishop F. C. Scott, and the executive board of the church had said that they wanted a church in Atlanta. The Brotherhood (The Church of the Living God leadership board) was supposed to help me financially and purchase a church building. In the mean time, Cinda and I labored in the field as 'tent-makers' (doing secular work to subsidize our church income). Still, we were struggling financially and the church's promises about financial support and purchasing a building never materialized. After months of broken promises, I decided to take the job offer in Los Angeles.

I worked in Los Angeles for three years before Bishop Jeff Ruffin, the district Bishop for the Church of the Living God (C.W.F.F.), offered me a church in Fresno, California. In order to supplement my income I began working as a chaplain with the Department of Veterans Affairs (VA). The chief of Chaplain Services, Colonel Donald Welsh, was also a chaplain in the Army Reserves.

It was not long before he asked me the $64,000 question; "Have you ever thought about becoming a chaplain in the military?" When I told him my story, he asked, "If I could help you get into the Army Reserves, would you consider it?" "Of course I would!" was my reply.

Chaplain Welsh made some calls and was able to help me with a "work around" to get an ecclesiastical endorsement and remain with the Church of the Living God. I would be endorsed by the National Evangelical Association which would serve as the umbrella for my Church. My Church officials agreed to this work around and on December 21, 1985, I took my oath of office and became a chaplain in the United States Army Reserves.

34

Chapter 5
Can I Be A Christian And A Soldier?

There are those who may question how I can be a Christian and a Soldier. Some actually express what many others think. "How can you be a man of peace and a man of war?" My answer is simple. I am a man of peace who does not discount the realities of war. And the God whom I serve *"is a man of war"* (Exodus 15:3).

The Bible's account of man's very existence on earth begins and ends with war.

When Moses wrote, *"In the beginning"* he was not talking about the beginning of time or even the beginning of earth. He was talking about the beginning of re-creation. God was starting over after having forcibly removed Satan from heaven. There was a war, an attempted coup actually, in heaven. Lucifer and a third of God's angels turned against their creator and Michael, the warring archangel who hovered over the throne of God, cast them down to the earth. Jesus said he " *beheld Satan as lightning fall from heaven."*

The beautiful story you read in Genesis 1, then, is actually the clean up effort after a battle.

The scriptures are replete with references to war.

War – *220*
Army / Armies – *116*
Soldier(s) – *33*
Centurion – *24*
Captain – *238*
Fight (fights / fighter / fighting / fighteth) – *111*
Sword(s) – *404*
Shield(s) – *65*
Spear(s) – *57*
Helmet(s) – *10*
Breastplate – *26*
Chariot(s) – *153*
Armour – *24*
Armourbearer -- *14*
Horsemen(3) – *56*
Footmen – *12*

Those 12 references to footmen, alone, represent 1.34 million troops. War is at the core of humanity.

People remember that Jesus said, *"Turn the other cheek."* But they forget that he also plaited a three-fold cord and drove the moneychangers out of the temple. They call Jesus the Prince of Peace. But they forget that he will return to judge the world with a flaming sword coming out of his mouth.

Our Lord said, *"from the days of John the Baptist until now the kingdom of heaven suffereth violence, and the violent take it by force"* Matthew 11:12.

Some of the most beloved characters in the scriptures were Soldiers.

David, who penned thousands of beautiful psalms, was, in fact, a warrior king. The women of Israel sang, *"Saul hath slain his thousands, and David his ten thousands"* (1 Samuel 18:7). There is not a metaphor in literature that has been used more than the battle between David and Goliath.

Deborah, the woman judge, killed a man by driving a hairpin through his temple. (**Note:** To this day, all Israeli citizens are considered members of the Israeli Army and Old Testament judges were consider ranking officers in that army.)

Samson, also a judge, ended his own life and fulfilled his destiny by slaying thousands of Philistines.

Samuel the prophet (actually all the prophets) accessorized his priestly garments with a sword. And part of his priestly duties consisted of killing or overseeing the death of the wicked.

"But all of that is Old Testament" you say.

It is true that the New Testament speaks of the grace and mercy of God. *"For God so loved the world, that he gave his only begotten Son, that whosoever believeth in him should not perish, but have everlasting life. For God sent not his Son into the world to condemn the world; but that the world through him might be saved"* (John 3:16,17). But let us not forget that neither the New Testament nor history ends with the gospels.

Romans 13:1-4 tells us that we should all *"be subject unto the higher powers. For there is no power but of God: the powers that be are ordained of God. Whosoever therefore resisteth the power, resisteth the ordinance of God: and they that resist shall receive to themselves damnation. For rulers are not a terror to good works, but to the evil. Wilt thou then not be afraid of the power? do that which is good, and thou shalt have praise of the same:"*

I find it especially interesting that Paul writes that the Soldier, the police officer, the warrior of this world is actually, *"the minister of God to thee for good."* And then Paul warns us, *"But if thou do that which is evil, be afraid; for he beareth not the sword in vain: for he is the minister of God, a revenger to execute wrath upon him that doeth evil."*

The truth is, people who struggle with Soldiers and war *"know not the scriptures, neither the power [the very nature] of God"* (Mark 12:24). They speak against war from the safety of homes, streets, and even pulpits that are protected by warriors. They look at the meekness of Jesus and mistake it for weakness. They forget that *"The Lord is not slack concerning his promise, as some men count slackness; but is longsuffering to us-ward, not willing that any should perish, but that all should come to repentance"* (2 Peter 3:9). In other words, God has declared a heavenly ceasefire hoping that you and yours will get it together, but the ceasefire is only temporary.

People forget that John the revelator *"saw heaven opened, and behold a white horse; and he that sat upon him was called Faithful and True, and in righteousness he doth judge and make war. His eyes were as a flame of fire, and on his head were many crowns; and he had a name written, that no man knew, but he himself. And he was clothed with a vesture dipped in blood: and his name is called The Word of God. And the armies which were in heaven followed him upon white horses, clothed in fine linen, white and clean. And out of his mouth goeth a sharp sword, that with it he should smite the nations: and he shall rule them with a rod of iron: and he treadeth the winepress of the fierceness and wrath of Almighty God. And he hath on his vesture and on his thigh a name written, KING OF KINGS, AND LORD OF LORDS"* (Revelation 19:11-16).

How can I be a Christian and a Soldier? Proudly. Though others forget, I remember that the Bible's account of man's very existence on earth begins and ends with war. I am proud to be called a Soldier, and even more so to have served the men and women who worship God and protect our freedoms every day.

Pro Deo Et Patria!

Mobilizing The Army of God

Chapter 6
The Chaplain

The office of the chaplain dates back to the fourth century, and fittingly, begins with a Soldier.

At the age of ten, Martin of Tours, a city in central France on the lower reaches of the river Loire, between Orléans and the Atlantic coast, defied his family and became a catechumen--a candidate for Christian baptism. Five years later and not yet baptized, as the son of a veteran officer, young Martin was required to join a cavalry.

While on garrison duty at the gates of the city of Amiens, about two hundred and forty miles north of Tours, Martin encountered a scantily clad beggar on a cold winter night. The Soldier reportedly took off his cloak, probably white lined with lamb's wool, and cut it in half with his sword. He gave half to the beggar and kept half for himself.

That night, Martin had a vision of Jesus Christ wearing the half cloak he had given to the beggar. Jesus said to the angels and the saints that surrounded him, "See! This is the mantle that Martin, yet a catechumen, gave me." When he woke, it was the "yet a catechumen" that encouraged Martin to be baptized immediately. He was eighteen years old.

Martin found it difficult to continue his military duties and carry on his new found faith, so he left the military just before a battle with the Gauls at Worms in 336. Martin determined that his faith prohibited him from fighting, saying, "I am a Soldier of Christ. I cannot fight." He was charged with cowardice and jailed, but in response to the charge, he volunteered to go, unarmed, to the front of the troops. But God had other plans. The battle never occurred and Martin was released from military service.

Martin became the patron saint of French kings in the Middle Ages. St. Martin's cloak (cappellanus) was carried into battle by the kings as a banner, signifying "the presence of God." Today, we might call it the anointing. Like Moses with the rod of God, when the anointed word is held high the people of God prevail. But when the ministers of the gospel grow weary and the anointed word hangs low, God's enemies prevail. (See Exodus 17).

Because the cloak was a sacred relic of the church, a priest went into battle with the king as the custodian of the cloak. The keeper of the cloak also attended to the King's spiritual needs. It was from this service that the office of the chaplain (from Medieval Latin cappellanus, from cappella) was birthed. The depository for the cloak became the chapel.

It is so like God that he would introduce me to the chaplaincy through singing *a capella* (in the style of the chapel) with the McMillans almost 1,600 years later. It is even more like God that Martin Luther was named after St. Martin. And Martin Luther King, Jr. was named after his father who was named after Martin Luther. And I was inspired to pursue the chaplaincy by a brief encounter with Dr. King as a young boy and a moving speech in tribute to Dr. King by a passionate chaplain when I, like Martin of Tours, was just a young Soldier.

I became the custodian of the cappellanus, the keeper of the cloak, the guardian of the covering--the angel of the anointing. I was given the glorious charge of attending to the spiritual needs of the king and his captains.

The story of St. Martin then, is more than a look at the origin of the term "chaplain". It gives us real insight into the true nature of the chaplaincy, as it is today. It gives us a glimpse of the purpose of ministry since ministry began. In the words of Moses' father-in-law, Jethro, the chaplain must, "Be...for the [Army] to God-ward," and "bring the causes unto God:" A good chaplain will, "teach them ordinances and laws, and...shew them the way wherein they must walk, and the work that they must do" (Exodus 18:19-20).

The chaplain, you see, was a member of one institution--the priesthood of the church, serving in another institution--the King's army. Priests have always anointed kings and kings have always consulted priests concerning God's wisdom and protection as they entered into business or battle. The US Army chaplaincy is no different. It was born of a combination of desire and need.

General George Washington had ministers to provide for his Continental Army as he battled the British. General Washington saw the need for men and women of faith and moral virtue as essential to good order and discipline in his unique military.

In their book, *Washington's God*, authors Michael and Jana Novak note, several times, the importance Washington placed on chaplains. About that Army, the Novaks say, "It is one of the least celebrated of Washington's accomplishments that he forged the first national peoples' Army in the world, whose structure and spirit had, 'no parallel in the annals of human revolution…no model on the face of the globe." The chaplaincy, in other words, was Washington's gift to his Army of freemen.

Although ministers served with the Continental Army, it would be years before an African-American would be commissioned as a chaplain. Henry Vinton Plummer was commissioned in 1884 as the first African-American Army chaplain. Captain Plummer served with the 9th Calvary Regiment--the famous Buffalo Soldiers--as a chaplain for ten years. Since then, many African-Americans have served men and women in uniform with honor.

I was privileged to join such a time-honored corp. At first, I was disappointed that I would not be an Air Force chaplain, but later I would come to appreciate the Army's approach to the chaplaincy.

For the Army, chaplaincy is 24/7 ministry in motion--serving those who serve. Unlike the Air force, whose chaplains at that time, remained at the base Chapel for the most part, the Army embedded their chaplains with the units. The chaplains did all the exercises with the troops. Wherever the troops went, the chaplain was there. I lived in tents and held field worship services. In Iraq, I used a Humvee to conduct Bible study. Wherever the troops were assigned, I was with them. We ate Meals Ready to Eat (MRE's) together. And

I was able to bring the presence, wisdom, and protection of God to meet their spiritual and natural needs.

Chapter 7
One Foot In Heaven

And how shall they preach, except they be sent?
as it is written, How beautiful are the feet of them
that preach the gospel of peace,
and bring glad tidings of good things!

Romans 10:15

It has been said that the chaplain, "has one foot in heaven and the other in a combat boot." Being an Army Reserve chaplain brought that truth to life for me, everyday for almost twenty-five years.

Army Reserve chaplains maintain a very busy dual life in parallel communities of faith. Many are pastors, serving local churches while they serve their nation's military. Generally, Reserve chaplains serve one weekend per month, in addition to three or four weeks of training throughout the year.

I, for example, served The Church of the Living God, (C.W.F.F.) Temple #12 in Fresno, California and reported to the nearest Army Reserve unit. I had, what I thought was, the best of both worlds--serving the men and women in uniform and serving the local community. The training I received in the Army as an officer, as a chaplain, and as a community pastor prepared me quite well for my next assignment.

Managing the lives of a pastor and a chaplain would not be as easy as I thought. I thank God I had an understanding wife and children. I missed a lot of special events, holidays and parenting moments. I couldn't have done it without an understanding wife and congregation. For years, people had to cope with their pastor not being there on some Sundays or during significant events. I also needed, and often had, an understanding commander.

Because Army Reserve chaplains have pastoral duties, there are times when they are not available 24/7. Some chaplains, for example, have to miss a half day from Sunday's battle assembly in order to be at their churches. Not all commanders understand this. They want their chaplain at the ready.

As you might imagine, the entire military went through a serious transition after September 11, 2001. Mobilization of forces in the Middle East demanded a more active role from the Reserves. Gradually, reservists like me found themselves giving much more of their time. That one week-end a month became a myth and we were spending more and more time with our units--training and preparing for probable deployment.

In some respects we wanted the opportunity to deploy and be 'active' Army for a period of time. That, after all, was what we trained so hard for year in and year out. At the same time, we knew the hardship this would cause for our families and employers. Employers for chaplains, more often than not, meant churches. Many chaplains deployed for a year and returned to find they did not have a church to pastor. My dual ministry for the most part would work together very well--until 1990, that is.

After accepting a charge to pastor a church in Los Angeles, I transferred from the 311th Station Hospital unit in Sharonville, Ohio to the 6218th USA Reception Battalion in Bell, California. The commander of that unit did not like the idea of me not being at the unit all day on Sundays. I tried to explain to him, as I had other commanders, that reserve chaplains who pastored had a Sunday commitment to their churches. I simply could not take the full day away from either committment on Sundays, so once a month I played Superman.

I would come to my unit in Bell, California for morning formation and sometimes for a morning worship service with the troops. Then, I would drive about fifteen miles, through heavy traffic, to my church in Los Angeles, change clothes, and preach to my congregation. Immediately after services I would go to my office and change back into my uniform and drive back to my unit for the afternoon. I spent those Sunday afternoons counseling or doing administrative work. After the closing formation, I would drive back to my church for evening services.

Although I always tried not to show any weariness to either my unit or my church, when I arrived home I would crash. I was thankful for an understanding wife and children. Although I did my best to juggle the two vocations, my commander gave me the two worst Officer Evaluation Reports (OER) of my military career. I can only pray that the Lord, my family, and my church were more gracious in their assessments of my performance during that period.

My prayers for relief were answered in 1992 when I was transferred to the 311th COSCOM, (a command support unit), in Los Angeles. I joined a team of chaplains who were very supportive of my pastoral duties. It was with this unit that I would be promoted to major and would have my first opportunity to be mobilized in 2004. The 311th COSCOM deployed with the 377th TSC (Tactical Support Command) out of Louisiana. I deployed with CH (COL) William Brunold who became the Command Chaplain of the TSC and I became the Command Chaplain of the Aerial Port of Debarkation (APOD) at Camp Doha, Kuwait.

Several services were offered in the chapel at Camp Doha. I began attending the 'Gospel' services. The gospel services are generally more charismatic and lively in worship style, and they typically last more than an hour, which is why most of them are the last worship service on Sunday. This one started at 1800 (6PM) on Sundays and would sometimes last until 2100 (9PM).

About a month after I was assigned to Camp Doha, the chaplain covering the gospel service, CH (LTC) Pearline Scott, was rotated back to the states and I would become the pastor for the gospel services. Unlike some of my colleagues, I loved to preach; I loved being involved in the worship experience of the Soldiers and civilians.

Being the APOD Command Chaplain and pastoring a congregation required putting in long hours. Many days, I would work and then counsel in the evening or lead Bible Studies and prayer groups.

Being a chaplain in a combat environment was very stress-ful--praying for convoys going into Iraq, riding in convoys to visits Soldiers, and receiving and giving final blessings to the remains at the mortuary affairs unit in Kuwait. My assignment at the Theatre Mortuary Evacuation Point (TMEP) was to work with the Soldiers who worked very professionally to make sure that they honored the fallen. The marines called their fallen "angels" and it was a honor to be a part of that process. We would call their names and read a scripture and give a prayer, then taps would be played as we rendered a salute.

At the beginning of my assignment at Camp Doha, I was assisting another chaplain with the gospel services. This was a time of great spiritual darkness in my life. I felt the darkness like a coat, and I could not shake it. While alone in my room, I could not even pray. The presence of demonic forces was palpable both in the region and on me personally. Remember, this was the part of the world where Daniel fasted and prayed while Michael the warrior archangel came to help dispatched messenger angels fight with the prince of Persia (Dan. 20:10-14).

I called my wife and aunt, Evangelist Alfreida Wynne, and asked them to pray for me. I also fasted and prayed for my spiritual breakthrough. I received my breakthrough during one of the gospel services. Actually, it was during a dance ministry that I experienced a deliverance from the spirit of heaviness.

I was a part of a team of Chaplains from various faith-groups. We protestant Chaplains provided spirited-worship services, including 'Revivals'. As far as I know, I was the first Chaplain to lead a revival service in Camp Arifjan, Kuwait and Camp Talil, Iraq.

During those revivals, with an emphasis on salvation and deliverance, many gave their lives to the Lord for the first time. Others rededicated their lives or experienced a powerful deliverance from their unhealthy habits. We even had baptisms in the desert. For many it was truly an 'Oasis in the Desert'--which was our vision statement. The experience strenghtened my faith because I was challenged to live what I preached in that setting, where eyes are on you 24/7, and what I've preached all my adult life about God's provision and protection.

It came down to, "Do you really believe this?" I was faced with many of the challenges of the other Soldiers. We endured separation from family and loved ones. And many of us wondered, "Will we live to see them again or will some crazed suicide bomber decide to end our lives in a dining facility we were eating in?

I am truly thankful that I was able to live an exemplary life of faith in a combat environment.

Chapter 8
A Farewell To Arms

To every thing there is a season,
and a time to every purpose under the heaven:

Ecclesiastes3:1

I am especially thankful for the many ministries that support the men and women in uniform who are deployed with various ministry resources.

Two of my spiritual fathers, Bishop Keith Butler and Dr. Bill Winston, sowed greatly into our lives. And Pastor Rick Warren of California really made a difference in the lives of our uniformed personnel with his book, *The Purpose Driven-Life*.

I was teaching 40 days of purpose with Rev. Jeff Moffett, a civilian pastor working as a contractor in Kuwait, when God gave me a vision and a mandate for Advancing His kingdom in the earth realm.

I knew that this vision was to make The Beloved Community--Dr. Martin Luther King, Jr.'s vision of a completely integrated society, a community of love and justice wherein brotherhood would be an actuality in all of social life--a reality in the twenty-first century. In Dr. King's mind, such a community would be the ideal corporate expression of the Christian faith.

God confirmed for me that my going to Kuwait was not just because I was deployed to support the Global War on Terrorism, but that I was on a 'Divine' assignment. My assignment from that moment on became to preach and teach the Kingdom of God and the currency of the Kingdom--faith.

I would serve a second tour of duty with the 311th ESC (Army Reserve Education Services Center) from April, 2008 through March, 2009, stationed at Camp Arfijan, Kuwait. During this deployment I was the Command Chaplain with the responsibility for most of Kuwait. The job was mostly administrative and focused on coordinating with our 'downtrace' units--units that answered to us as higher Headquarters for religious coverage--including (TMEP). Again, I found my greatest joy in pastoring the gospel services from June 2008 through March 2009.

Pastoring the gospel services was very demanding. Some Sundays, the attendance was over 300. I was blessed to have a Soldier and a civilian to serve as my executive pastors. Sargeant First Class Charles Anderson, an ordained elder, served until he redeployed. He was followed by Ms. Beverly McLain, a contract civilian and also an ordained elder. They both helped me with a lot of the administrative duties of pastoring the gospel services.

God gave me a message about harvesting souls for the Kingdom and He emphasized that revival starts with the individual. We subsequently held a revival at Camp Arifjan from October 1-3, 2008. The theme was "Ushering In The End Time Harvest." Those who attended were ministered to by chaplains from nearby Camps Victory and Virginia. Topics included: "Jesus Christ is the Answer for the World", "Fruits of the Holy Spirit", and "What's In A Name".

Approximately 650 service members and civilians attended the event and over 30 responded to the altar calls for salvation or rededication. Thirty-three were baptized the following Sunday in the pool.

The baptism services were very anointed. There was singing and we experienced a mighty move of the Holy Spirit. During one of the baptism services two bystanders were moved to be baptized on the spot. Glory be to God!

A personal highlight of my deployment to Kuwait was a surprise visit from my wife for my farewell celebration. My dear friends David and Brenda Graham, contract civilians I met during my first tour in Kuwait, orchestrated this feat and not without some disturbance in the higher command of Camp Arifjan. But my General, Brigadier General William Frink stood by me, and after an investigation, all ended well.

After a week's visit, my wife returned home to California and I was able to help our unit complete a very successful mission. We soon made our way home, with no loss of life, to God be the glory.

In July, 2009, my Army career would come to an end. My unit gave me a most excellent farewell. I proudly wore my dress blues with all my ribbons, recognizing my service and personal accomplishments as a member of the United States armed forces. They included:

The Meritorious Service Medal, The Army Commendation Medal, The Army Achievement Medal w/3 oak leafs, The Air Force Good conduct Medal, The Army Reserve Components Achievement Medal (5th award), The National Defense Service Medal (2nd award), The Global War on Terrorism Medal, The Armed Forces Reserve Medal (with bronze hourglass and "M" device), The Armed Forces Reserve Medal and The Army Service Ribbon.

During my retirement ceremony, my commander, Brigadier General William Frink, presented me with the Legion of Merit Medal.

This award brought tears to my eyes. This coupled with the kind words and expressions of gratitude made this day unforgettable. I can say without hesitation, it was the apex of a long and tedious climb. And I enjoyed the journey.

I coined a phrase which I repeated at many formations, when called upon to give a thought for the day. I would often start off by saying, "It's a great day to be alive, and a great day to be in the Army!" I would always get a loud, "HOOHA!!!"

THE LEGION OF MERIT
TO LIEUTENANT COLONEL MILTON S. HERRING
63rd Regional Readiness Command

For exceptionally meritorious service in position of in-creasing responsibility, culminating a 29-year career as chaplain, 311th Sustainment Command, 63rd Regional Readiness Command. Lieutenant Colonel Herring pro-vided unparalleled support and dedication to multiple Command Master Religious Programs and Unit Ministry Teams throughout The Army Reserve.

His exemplary service and commitment to the nation through times of both war and peace were steadfast and unwavering. His devotion to our Nation's Soldier, their families, and the mission is his legacy. Upon retirement, Lieutenant Colonel Herring is recognized for distin-guished performance of duty that represents exemplary achievement in the finest traditions of the United States Army. From: 20 July, 1999 to 19 July 2009.

This 1st day of July 2009
BY ORDER OF THE SECRETARY OF THE ARMY

The Army Chaplain
by Elizabeth F. Clark

Pray for the Chaplain, Mother,
As the Chaplain prays for your son.
He gave us the strength and the courage.
It was through his faith that we won.
His is the role that is hardest, for
He must believe through the Hell
Of the murdering missiles of war,
And give comfort to those that they fell.

We, who were picked for this 'action'
Who had been trained and hardened by drill,
We, were schooled in the art of fighting,
Were coached in the methods to kill.
Yet he, who had opposite teaching
Who had learned to be humble and kind,
It was to him we turned before battle
During the wait that shatters the mind.

Then in the midst of the fighting,
He was cool, calm, self-possessed.
His was the glorious winning,
Ours, but a bloody conquest.
For he braved the worst of the firing,
To give comfort to those in need.
Giving spiritual aid to the dying,
No matter their race, nor their creed.

We fighters will be rewarded by medals,
Our victory with praises be sung.
We'll live in the pages of history.
Our deeds will be taught to the young.
But, pray for the Chaplain, Mother.
Please God, may his reward be great.
He was truly the winner.
He fought with love against hate.

 58

The Vision

Chapter 9
Advancing
The Kingdom of God

But seek ye first the kingdom of God, and his
righteousness; and all these things shall be added unto you.

Matthew 6:33

The Kingdom of God is the rule of God, the reign of God. It
is conducting the business of God His way.

In 2004 while I was deployed to Kuwait as an Army chaplain
in support of the Global War on Terrorism, God gave me a
mandate for Advancing the Kingdom of God in the earth
realm. This vision is to make the 'Beloved Community' a
reality in the twenty-first century.

During my time in Kuwait, I had the opportunity to visit
various parts of the country and I made several observations.
As God was ministering to me about His Kingdom, He used
the Kuwaiti people as a living object lesson. He used their
lifestyle to show me how to live kingdom-minded.

Kuwait is a sovereign Arab emirate situated in the northeast of the Arabian Peninsula in Western Asia. It is bordered by Saudi Arabia to the south and Iraq to the north and lies on the northwestern shore of the Persian Gulf. It is slightly larger that Hawaii.

Kuwait is a constitutional monarchy with a parliamentary system of government, very much like the United Kingdom. A monarch acts as head of state within the parameters of a constitution. Kuwait has been ruled by the al-Sabah family since 1756.

In the year 1899, Kuwait entered into a treaty with the United Kingdom that gave the British extensive control over the foreign policy of Kuwait in exchange for protection and annual subsidy. Soon after the start of World War I, the British invalidated the convention and declared Kuwait an independent principality under the protection of the British Empire. And on 19 June 1961, Kuwait became fully independent following an exchange of notes between the United Kingdom and the then Amir of Kuwait, Abdullah III Al-Salim Al-Sabah.

For years the Kuwaiti people were an obscure people, either herding sheep or fishing and diving for pearls. Then something happened to change their mindset and their lifestyle. Oil was discovered in Kuwait in the 1930's, and Kuwait proved to have 20% of the world's known oil resources.

The sheik, who receives half of the profits, devotes most of the resources to education, welfare, and modernization of his kingdom. Those who are full-blooded Kuwaiti are taken care of by the Emir, the crown prince.

In 2007 unemployment was 2.2%, inflation was 5%, and non-Kuwaitis represented about 80% of the labor force.

As I moved around the country of Kuwait, I noticed that the Kuwaiti people carried themselves like royalty. They talked, dressed, drove, lived like they belonged to a kingdom. These once desert-dwellers now had an air of sophistication about them.

God showed me that this is how He expects His children to carry themselves, like King's kids, like royalty, like He really IS our source and provider. While the Kuwaiti are Muslims advancing their agenda throughout the world, we must be about our Father's business--advancing His kingdom in the earth.

God's word to us in Deuteronomy 8:18 is crystal clear. *"And you shall remember the Lord your God, for it is He who gives you power to get wealth, that He may establish His covenant which He swore to your fathers, as it is this day."*

This is wealth with a mission. This is wealth for a purpose. We have a greater resource inside of us that we must tap into. And like our Kuwaiti cousins, we too must develop a kingdom mind-set. We must come to see ourselves as royal kings and priests operating in the earth. We have destiny on the inside of us, and this is our season.

Like a mighty army whose time has come, it is the church's time to shine! Let's mobilize an army for God and advance His righteous cause in every arena of society.

The vision the Lord gave me was becoming clearer. And while I knew that there were other areas of focus, my initial focus was on Kingdom government, Kingdom economics, and Kingdom education. Also, I knew my mission would always have an emphasis on ministry to the military.

Later, I began to hear one of my spiritual fathers, Dr. Bill Winston, teach on the 'Kingdom of God' and I gained more insight. I shared my budding vision with my wife and later she read a book by Johnny Enlow, *The Seven Mountain Prophecy*.

In his book, Enlow referenced three other men--Lance Wallnau, Loren Cunningham, and Bill Bright. Lance Wallnau and his teaching on the 'Seven Mountain Strategy' once shared how Loren Cunningham of Youth With a Mission (YWAM) was scheduled for a lunch meeting with Bill Bright in 1972. As they were on their way to lunch with each other, the Lord separately gave Cunningham and Bright the same revelation of a "seven-mountain strategy."

In this revelation, the Lord told them that there were seven mountains, or kingdoms, to dominate--seven mind-molders of society. The Lord instructed each of them to tell the other this message, along with an important promise: "Capture these mountains, and you'll capture the nation."

Psalm 2:8 resonated in my spirit as I read the account of their divine revelation. While the vision began with three areas, I knew, somehow, there were others to be included in this end-time Kingdom message. It is a strategy for us as faithful believers in the Lord Jesus Christ to carry out the Great Commission which we read in both Mark's and Matthew's gospel.

From my years in the military both as an enlistee in the Air Force and as an officer in the Army, I knew that God was calling me to mobilize an Army that would advance His kingdom in the earth.

We held our first Advancing The Kingdom Of God Conference in Atlanta, Georgia in 2005 and included a 'Ministry to the Military' event. The ministry to the military event is an opportunity for civilians to show their appreciation for those serving in the armed forces and an opportunity for those in the armed forces to share testimonies about their faith in uniform. I know, first hand, from my two deployments in Kuwait, that many lives are changed and transformed for the glory of God while they are serving in the desert.

Advancing the Kingdom of God is about preaching, teaching, and implementing the Gospel of the Kingdom. In the next few chapters, I want to make plain my vision and clarify just what the gospel of the Kingdom is and why it is so important.

Mobilizing The Army of God

Chapter 10

The Gospel of
The Kingdom

First of all, the gospel of the kingdom is what Jesus came to reveal to mankind.

> *"Now after that John was put in prison, Jesus came into Galilee, preaching the gospel of the kingdom of God, And saying, The time is fulfilled, and the kingdom of God is at hand: repent ye, and believe the gospel."*

Mark 1:14-15

The synoptic Gospels and the book of Acts make at least twenty direct references to the preaching of *"the gospel of the kingdom."* Here are just a few (Kingdom references are bold for emphasis.):

> *In those days came John the Baptist, preaching in the wilderness of Judaea, And saying, Repent ye: for **the kingdom of heaven** is at hand.* Matthew 3:1-2

*And this **gospel of the kingdom** shall be preached in all the world for a witness unto all nations; and then shall the end come.* Matthew 24:14

*Then he called his twelve disciples together, and gave them power and authority over all devils, and to cure diseases. And he sent them to **preach the kingdom of God**, and to heal the sick.* Luke 9:1-2

*And he said unto them, Go ye into all the world, and **preach the gospel to every creature**. He that believeth and is baptized shall be saved; but he that believeth not shall be damned.*

And these signs shall follow them that believe; In my name shall they cast out devils; they shall speak with new tongues; They shall take up serpents; and if they drink any deadly thing, it shall not hurt them; they shall lay hands on the sick, and they shall recover. Mark 16:15-18

*The former treatise have I made, O Theophilus, of all that Jesus began both to do and teach, Until the day in which he was taken up, after that he through the Holy Ghost had given commandments unto the apostles whom he had chosen: To whom also he shewed himself alive after his passion by many infallible proofs, being seen of them forty days, and **speaking of the things pertaining to the kingdom of God:***

And, being assembled together with them, commanded them that they should not depart from Jerusalem, but wait for the promise of the Father, which, saith he, ye have heard of me. For John truly baptized with water; but ye shall be baptized with the Holy Ghost not many days hence.

When they therefore were come together, they asked of him, saying, Lord, wilt thou at this time restore again the kingdom to Israel? And he said unto them, It is not for you to know the times or the seasons, which the Father hath put in his own power.

But ye shall receive power, after that the Holy Ghost is come upon you: and ye shall be witnesses unto me both in Jerusalem, and in all Judaea, and in Samaria, and unto the uttermost part of the earth. Acts 1:1-8

This kingdom message was certainly the message of the early church. Here are a few more references from the book of Acts. (Kingdom references are bold for emphasis.)

*But when they believed Philip **preaching the things concerning the kingdom of God**, and the name of Jesus Christ, they were baptized, both men and women.* Acts 8:12

*And he went into the synagogue, and spake boldly for the space of three months, disputing and persuading the **things concerning the kingdom of God**.* Acts 19:8

69

*And now, behold, I know that ye all, among whom **I have gone preaching the kingdom of God**, shall see my face no more.* Acts 20:25

*And when they had appointed him a day, there came many to him into his lodging; to whom he expounded and **testified the kingdom of God**, persuading them concerning Jesus, both out of the law of Moses, and out of the prophets, from morning till evening.* Acts 28:23

*And Paul dwelt two whole years in his own hired house, and received all that came in unto him, **Preaching the kingdom of God**, and teaching those things which concern the Lord Jesus Christ, with all confidence, no man forbidding him.* Acts 28:30-31

The word 'Gospel' is an incredibly powerful word. The gospel is, in fact, *"the power of God unto salvation..."* (Romans 1:16). Gospel means good news. And the word 'news' denotes a reporting of recent events or the revealing of previously unknown information about something that has already taken place.

So, Jesus came to report or reveal something good that had (has) already taken place--something we didn't know about. Jesus came to tell us that the Kingdom has been restored to the way it was in the Garden of Eden. Jesus came to tell us that the time between when man fell and when he was redeemed has been fulfilled, and the Kingdom is literally *at hand*--reachable, obtainable, inhabitable. The kingdom is here now! All mankind needed to do in order to see and enter the Kingdom was repent and believe.

 70

Jesus answered and said unto him, Verily, verily, I say unto thee, Except a man be born again, he cannot see the kingdom of God. John 3:3

Jesus answered, Verily, verily, I say unto thee, Except a man be born of water and of the Spirit, he cannot enter into the kingdom of God. John 3:5

Now, repent has been defined as becoming Godly sorrowful for one's sins and making a decision to turn from them. That is a great definition. But there is another definition, one that I believe fits better when talking about the Kingdom. If we break the word repent into its two syllables, 're' means to do over or go back to, and 'pent' speaks of things that are higher as in penthouse. Therefore, repent could mean to return to a higher place--your highest place.

The Kingdom of God represents the place you held before the fall of Adam and Eve. Both of these definitions require us to be transformed in our way of thinking. That's why Paul the apostle reminded you to be *"transformed by the renewing of your mind"* (Romans 12:2).

To believe is to place one's full weight, one's full trust, one's total reliance upon someone or something. In other words, Jesus is saying that we have been restored to our rightful place, the place that Adam was in before the fall. Jesus our redeemer has come and in order for us to see and enter into the Kingdom all we need to do is make a shift in our thinking, see ourselves as God sees us and put our complete faith and trust in Jesus.

This may challenge your thinking, but the gospel of the Kingdom is actually more than the gospel of salvation. The gospel of salvation is, in fact, only a small part of the gospel of the kingdom. Let's compare the two gospels.

The gospel of Salvation focuses primarily on the part of eternity we will enjoy after this life. The gospel of the Kingdom, on the other hand, includes the parts of eternity that we are experiencing now.

The gospel of Salvation expresses a concern for individual souls. The gospel of the Kingdom focuses on nations. The gospel of Salvation focuses primarily on things that are sacred--justification, sanctification, holiness, etc.... The gospel of the Kingdom treats both the sacred and secular as one.

The gospel of Salvation has a view toward heaven, while the gospel of the Kingdom aims to make heaven's glory visible on earth. Hence, Jesus' instruction to his disciples to pray *"Thy kingdom come, Thy will be done in earth, as it is in heaven"* (Matthew 6:10).

The invisible (heavenly) kingdom must be manifested in the earth. And contrary to popular belief, the Kingdom does not pertain to buildings, bricks and mortar. Jesus made this clear in Luke 17:20b-21 when he said, *"The kingdom of God cometh not with observation: Neither shall they say, Lo here! or, lo there! for, behold, the kingdom of God is within you."*

We did not get born again just to go to heaven. The thought of going to heaven may be reassuring, but the kingdom of God is here and now.

The gospel of the Kingdom asks, "Now that you have been born again, what is your purpose? What is your assignment? Which mountain or sphere are you called to take? The gospel of the Kingdom gives you a passion for nations. The gospel of the Kingdom makes you want to show forth God's glory here in the earth realm.

The gospel of the Kingdom also teaches us that we have a vital role to play in helping to hasten the return of Jesus. Remember, Jesus said, *"...this "gospel of the Kingdom will be preached in all the world as a witness to all nations, and then the end will come"* (Matthew 24:14).

Chapter 11

Why Is This So Important?

Why is this message so important? Because when we teach, preach, and implement strategies for taking the seven mountains I mentioned in chapter 8, endeavoring to transform a culture, we are actually carrying out the great commission Jesus gave in Matthew 28:18-20 and Mark 16: 15-18. One might say our goal, then, is to fulfill the prophecy of Isaiah 2:2.

> *"Now it shall come to pass in the latter days,"* it reads, *"that the mountain of the Lord's house shall be established on the top of the mountains, and shall be exalted above the hills, and all nations shall flow to it."*

In the fifth chapter of The Revelation, we get a glimpse into an amazing moment taking place in heaven. The Father is on His throne and He holds in His right hand a scroll with seven seals that no one has been found worthy to loose. John the apostle is overcome with sadness and tears as he contemplates this heavenly reality, when an elder comes to John and tells him not to weep because someone has just shown up who IS worthy to *"open the book, and to loose the seven seals thereof"* (Revelation 5:5).

This someone is the Lamb who was slain for the sins of the world! He is described as *"having seven horns and seven eyes, which are the seven Spirits of God sent forth into all the earth"* (Revelation 5:6). This Someone is Jesus.

The *"seven horns"* represents seven foundations of power that the Lamb has because of His awesome act of redemption on the cross. In other words, the Last Adam, Jesus, regained everything the first Adam abdicated, including the authority to establish the rule of God upon the seven gates, or spheres or mountains, which exist in every culture in the earth.
Once Jesus takes the book out of his Father's hand, the twenty-four elders begin singing a *'new'* song.

Thou art worthy to take the book
and to open the seals thereof
for thou wast slain
and hast redeemed us to God by thy blood
out of every kindred, and tongue
and people, and nation
And hast made us unto our God
kings and priests
and we shall reign on the earth

Then the entire heavenly host shouted; *"Worthy is the Lamb that was slain to receive power, and riches, and wisdom, and strength, and honour, and glory, and blessing"* (Revelation 5:12). Each of the seven attributes of majesty that Jesus is worthy to receive speaks directly to one of the seven mountains of every nation's culture or society

1. Power speaks of Government
2. Riches speak of Economy
3. Wisdom speaks of Education
4. Strength speaks of Family
5. Honor speaks of Religion
6. Glory speaks of Celebration (Arts and Entertainment)
7. Blessing speaks of Media

The great commission, given by Jesus, in Matthew 28:19, is to *"make disciples of all the nations."* We are charged to make Revelation 11:15 a reality. *"The Kingdoms of this world have become the kingdoms of our Lord and His Christ, and He shall reign forever and ever!"*

God is mobilizing an army of priests and kings, an army of servants in relationship with Jesus Christ as Supreme Commander. Using the seven mountain paradigm, we are challenging believers to dominate every mountain and in so doing the Lord's house will be established on the top of each one.

Let me focus on one of the mountains using the template Johnny Enlow presents in his book, *The Seven Mountain Prophecy.* Let's look at the mountain of economy.

This mountain can also be called the mountain of wealth or money. In order to understand this template let's first look at Enlow's Biblical references to the seven mountains and see how he identifies 'the enemy' of each of the mountains.

Each mountain has its own principalities, its own significant displacing authority. There are aerial adversaries assigned to each mountain, determined to sabotage the basic mission of each mountain.

In Deuteronomy 7:1 we read, *"When the Lord your God brings you into the land which you go to possess and has cast out many nations before you, the Hittites and the Girgashite and the Amorites and the Canaanite and the Perizzites and the Hivites and the Jebusites, seven nations greater and mightier than you."* Enlow gives the revelation that these seven nations represent the infrastructural columns of our societies and that it is the Lord's plan to raise His people up to rule every social, economic, and political structure of our nations.

These mountains are: media, government, education, economy, religion, celebration of arts and entertainment, and family and social service.

Michael E. Evans, in his book, *Return Of The Lazarus Generation,* identifies "seven pillars of the community that are critical to the recovery of failed people, especially ex-offenders." Compare Evans' list to Enlow's and an amazing pattern appears.

Evans	Enlow
1. family, friends & neighbors	*family and social service*
2. churches & faith based organizations	*religion*
3. clubs & associations	*arts and entertainment*
4. schools, colleges & universities	*education*
5. businesses	*economy*
6. the media (broadcast, print, electronic)	*media*
7. government & civil servants	*government*

"These seven sectors of society," says Evans, "form a circle of influence that can be used to keep people out of the community or help them back in."

Enlow's book was published in January 2008. Evans' book was published in June of the same year. According to Evans, the two had never met and Evans was completely unaware of Enlow's revelation. Apparently, God is speaking to many about the need to take these mountains.

The strategy for taking these mountains is part prayer and part action. The five-fold ministry plays an important part, as well. The gift of the Prophet and the prophetic word are especially important because God announces everything He does before He does it. *"Surely the Lord GOD will do nothing, but he revealeth his secret unto his servants the prophets"* (Amos 3:7).

The mountain of economy is represented in Deuteronomy 7 by the Canaanites. The Canaanite represents the love of money. The Promised Land was often called Canaan and we know it was a land flowing with milk and honey. Milk and honey are evidence of fruitfulness, productivity, and prosperity. Canaan and its inhabitants, therefore, represent a form of economic boom.

'Canaanite,' in Hebrew, can be translated as merchant, or trader. It can also mean "to be humbled, brought low, or to be under subjection." The word 'Cana' actually means zealous. Together, these words paint a sordid picture of greed and poverty. The Canaanites on this mountain of economic boom are working to either get people to be over zealous in their trading and merchandizing or to subject them to poverty, or both. These Canaanites of greed and poverty are diametrically opposed to anyone living in and relying on God's provision.

One of God's names is Jehovah-Jireh--*The Lord my provider.* When people buy into the Canaanites' philosophy, they don't see God as their provider and they live under either the banner of financial hopelessness or the banner of financial excess. It's feast or famine; spend baby spend, shop until you drop, or I can barely make it to pay day, brother can you spare a dime? No wonder we are always 'charging' to the malls.

When we choose Jehovah-Jireh, we choose to live under the banner of the the Lord's provision. As individuals, we need to scale this mountain. As a church, we must dominate this mountain. We must become debt-free, responsible stewards of God's finances. We must honor God with our first fruits, tithes and offerings and learn to trust Him as our source and resource because *"...the love of money* [whether you have any or not] *is the root of all evil: which while some coveted after, they have erred from the faith, and pierced themselves through with many sorrows."* (I Tim. 6:10).

As followers of Jesus Christ we have been commissioned in the Army of God to implement the General Order given in Matthew 28:18-20. The order includes making disciples of all nations (v.19). The question, then, must be raised, "Just how do you disciple a nation?" The answer to the question is more than getting an individual to say yes to Jesus as their Lord, Savior and Liberator, although this is the first step. A nation is discipled by every born again believer having an influential voice in each of the seven spheres/mountains that shape every society. It takes money to carry out this order. This is what is called, "Money with a mission".

I am calling on believers in this mighty Army or move of God to become "disentangled" from this present world system and to embrace a life-changing commitment to God's (Kingdom) system. The Kingdom of God is the rule of God, or God's way of conducting business.

Ascending to the top of our economic mountain means having what is called in the military, 'situational awareness' of the spiritual activities which surround this mountain. These activities are what the Apostle Paul refers to as 'principalities' in heavenly places.

Mobilizing The Army of God

Chapter 12
Principalities

*"For we do not wrestle against flesh and blood,
but against principalities, against powers, against rulers
of the darkness of this age, against spiritual hosts of
wickedness in the heavenly places."*

Ephesians 6:12

It is precisely because *"...the love of money* [whether you
have any or not] *is the root of all evil:"* that we must be
keenly aware of Satan and his cohorts in monetary arenas.

People read newspapers and watch markets believing that
upswings and downturns are purely a function of human behavior. Job loss. Deficits. Tax shifts. Natural disasters.
But scriptural history teaches us that other forces are at play.
Kingdoms are established and destroyed in the heavens long
before we see the earthly outcomes.

In Chapter 7, I made reference to the prince of Persia who
withstood Daniel for twenty-one days. Some of the same
princes are resisting us, too. Don't take my word for it, read
it for yourself.

"But the prince of the kingdom of Persia withstood me one and twenty days: but, lo, Michael, one of the chief princes, came to help me; and I remained there with the kings of Persia" (Daniel 10:13).

The prince of Persia is a principality, a satanic spirit, a fallen angel, who rules over that part of the world. There are principalities ruling over each of the seven mountains, also. The principality or the king of the economy mountain is Mammon or Babylon. Mammon is the Syrian god of riches. Mammon is also a term used to personify greed and unjust worldly gain.

Jesus warned us that *"No servant can serve two masters: for either he will hate the one, and love the other; or else he will hold to the one, and despise the other. Ye cannot serve God and mammon"* (Luke 16:13).

Babylon also represents the world system. John, the revelator described Babylon this way:

> *"And after these things I saw another angel come down from heaven, having great power; and the earth was lightened with his glory. And he cried mightily with a strong voice, saying, Babylon the great is fallen, is fallen, and is become the habitation of devils, and the hold of every foul spirit, and a cage of every unclean and hateful bird. For all nations have drunk of the wine of the wrath of her fornication, and the kings of the earth have committed fornication with her, and the merchants of the earth are waxed rich through the abundance of her delicacies"* (Revelation 18:1-3).

Since the Garden of Eden, Satan has looked for flaws in the human character and targeted dominant human passions in an ongoing effort to undermine God's plan for man.

In Genesis 3, he capitalized on the lust of the flesh, the lust of the eyes and the pride of life in Eve. He encouraged her to look on the tree of the knowledge of good and evil and ultimately enticed her to disobey God and eat. Adam followed, eyes wide open, and sold us all into sin.

God responded to Satan's attack with a promise to destroy Satan and redeem mankind. *"And I will put enmity between thee and the woman,"* God declared, *"and between thy seed and her seed; it shall bruise thy head, and thou shalt bruise his heel"* (Genesis 3:15). Satan took the bait and began to attack human sexuality.

"And it came to pass, when men began to multiply on the face of the earth, and daughters were born unto them, That the sons of God saw the daughters of men that they were fair; and they took them wives of all which they chose" (Genesis 6:1). Angels have the ability to take on human form. (See Hebrews 13:2) Satan, knowing this, sent fallen angels in the form of men to marry and multiply with human females. Of these unions, giants were born.

"There were giants in the earth in those days; and also after that, when the sons of God [fallen angels] *came in unto the daughters of men, and they bare children to them, the same ι ᴢcame mighty men which were of old, men of renown"* (Genesis 6:4). Something far more ominous was born of those satanic unions. Satan's deception coupled with man's disobedience, birthed the wrath of God against humanity.

Modern meteorologists might have called Noah's flood a natural disaster. Some even dare to call such cataclysms, 'Acts of God.' The truth is, these so called natural disasters are God's response to man's actions born of Satan's influence. Principalities are continually controlling and toppling kingdoms.

It was the devil that influenced Pharaoh to murder the male children of the Israelites in the days of Moses. Satan knew that God's chosen people, the people who would one day produce Messiah, had cried out to God for a deliverer. Their cries, undoubtedly, passed through the heavens and the princes of the power of the air over Egypt heard them. Moses had no contemporaries because principalities provoked men to destroy his playmates.

The same thing happened when Jesus was born. Wise men from the east followed a star to Bethlehem to worship the newborn king. Herod caught wind of their pilgrimage and inquired about the birthday of Jesus. When he realized that the child was approximately two years old, he was led of the devil to kill all children up to two years of age. The guiding star was in the heavens and so were the principalities, *"wandering stars,"* (Jude 13) that motivated the massacre. When Jesus was raised from the dead, Mammon, the prince of greed and unjust worldly gain, raised his head again.

Many believe it was Mary who first witnessed and declared the resurrection of Jesus, but she was not. When Jesus was laid in the tomb of Joseph of Arimathaea, the Pharisees knew that Jesus had told the disciples he would rise from the dead so they said to Pontius Pilate, *"Sir, we remember that that deceiver said, while he was yet alive, After three days I will rise again. Command therefore that the sepulchre be made sure until the third day, lest his disciples come by night, and steal him away, and say unto the people, He is risen from the dead: so the last error shall be worse than the first"*

Pilate took their advice and told his soldiers, *"Ye have a watch: go your way, make it as sure as ye can."* And the Bible says, *"they went, and made the sepulchre sure, sealing the stone, and setting a watch"* (Matthew 27:63-66).

Three days later, the stone that had covered the tomb was rolled back and the body of Jesus was gone. The Roman guards knew they were dead men, having lost their charge. But they also knew they hadn't left their posts. They knew, and testified that God had surely raised Jesus from the dead.

The scriptures say, *"some of the watch* [the guards] *came into the city, and shewed unto the chief priests all the things that were done."* Enter the spirit of Mammon, knowing that if people believe Jesus is risen, power shifts and fortunes are lost. The same thing happened when Lazarus was raised from the dead. (See John 12:10-11)

"And when they were assembled with the elders, and had taken counsel, they gave large money unto the soldiers, Saying, Say ye, His disciples came by night, and stole him away while we slept. And if this come to the governor's ears, we will persuade him, and secure you" (Matthew 28:11-14).

Once again, the princes of the power of the air moved men to resist God. They paid them not to tell the world that Jesus was risen. The Bible says, *"they took the money, and did as they were taught: and this saying is commonly reported among the Jews until this day"* (Matthew 28:15). How many men, because of satanically inspired avarice, greed, and lust, have denied the Lord who died for them and shut their mouths in the face of injustice, immorality, and deceit?

I have emphasized the satanic activity, but don't forget God's consistent victory. Truly, He *"always causeth us to triumph in Christ, and maketh manifest the savour of his knowledge by us in every place"* (2 Corinthians 2:14).

"These things I have spoken unto you," God says, *"that in me ye might have peace. In the world ye shall have tribulation: but be of good cheer; I have overcome the world"* (John 16:33).

He admonishes us to *"be not conformed to this world: but be ye transformed by the renewing of your mind, that ye may prove what is that good, and acceptable, and perfect, will of God"* (Rom.12:2).

We are further warned, to *"Love not the world, neither the things that are in the world. If any man love the world,"* God says, *"the love of the Father is not in him. For all that is in the world, the lust of the flesh, and the lust of the eyes, and the pride of life, [the same passions that Satan used against Eve] is not of the Father, but is of the world"* (1 John 2:15-16)

Revelation 18 speaks of a time when the economic system of this world will collapse. Wealth itself will not collapse, but the present system of trader (Canannite) domination will.

"And after these things I saw another angel come down from heaven, having great power; and the earth was lightened with his glory. And he cried mightily with a strong voice, saying, Babylon the great is fallen, is fallen, and is become the habitation of devils, and the hold of every foul spirit, and a cage of every unclean and hateful bird. For all nations have drunk of the wine of the wrath of her fornication, and the kings of the earth have committed fornication with her, and the merchants of the earth are waxed rich through the abundance of her delicacies"

The merchants of the earth are traders, businesspeople, those who buy and sell. Fornication, by definition is unfaithfulness or infidelity. It is a form of fornication for anyone to look to anyone other than God for provision. God's warning to His people, then, is *"Come out of her, my people, that ye be not partakers of her sins, and that ye receive not of her plagues. For her sins have reached unto heaven, and God hath remembered her iniquities"* (Revelation 18:1-5)

Since the tower of Babel (Genesis 6), Babylon has been associated with the confusion of mixing. Centers of commerce have always drawn people from differing cultures and backgrounds together. Men will cross barriers of every kind to get to a dollar. Jesus died to break down the middle wall of partition and make us one new man, but Babylon serves a seductive wine, and even God's people can be intoxicated by it.

Mammon and Babylon represent the power atop this mountain of wealth, and that spirit must be dispossessed.

Chapter 13
The Prophet

"...the children of Issachar, ...were men that had under-standing of the times, to know what Israel ought to do;"

1 Chronicles 12:32

Identifying an enemy is one thing. Knowing how to defeat him is another thing altogether. In the military, we had covert operatives, unmanned intelligence gathering drones, and even outright spies. Espionage is a powerful weapon that all Soldiers value. But espionage has its limits, (Reference news reports as recent as June 30, 2010.)

On June 27, 2010, 10 people in Yonkers, Boston and northern Virginia were arrested and accused of being part of a Russian espionage ring, living under false names and deep cover in a patient scheme to penetrate what one coded message called American "policy making circles." The next day, an 11th accused member of the ring was arrested at an airport in Cyprus while trying to leave for Budapest.

The armies of God have an even more powerful intelligence gathering method. I'm talking about the Prophets. Jesus gave us a powerful gift called the five-fold ministry. *"And he gave some, apostles; and some, prophets; and some, evangelists; and some, pastors and teachers"* (Ephesians 4:11). And one of those ministries can give us a great advantage over our spiritual adversaries. The Prophets can tell us what we need to do. Let's take a look at a prophet in action.

> *Then the king of Syria warred against Israel, and took counsel with his servants, saying, In such and such a place shall be my camp.*
>
> *And the man of God sent unto the king of Israel, saying, Beware that thou pass not such a place; for thither the Syrians are come down.*
>
> *And the king of Israel sent to the place which the man of God told him and warned him of, and saved himself there, not once nor twice.*
>
> *Therefore the heart of the king of Syria was sore troubled for this thing; and he called his servants, and said unto them, Will ye not shew me which of us is for the king of Israel?*
>
> *And one of his servants said, None, my lord, O king: but Elisha, the prophet that is in Israel, telleth the king of Israel the words that thou speakest in thy bedchamber.* 2 Kings 6:8-12

God used the prophet to warn his people, not once, not twice, but as often as was needed, so that they would know how to defeat their enemies.

A prophet is one who speaks what God is speaking. The Hebrew word that is translated "to prophesy" means to flow forth. It can best be described as "to bubble forth like a fountain, to let drop, to lift up, or to spring forth."

The Greek word, "to prophesy" means to speak for another. In this case, it means to speak for God or to be His spokesman. The prophet, then, is given to bring revelation to his generation.

It was the prophet Jeremiah who let us know that God knows *"the thoughts that* [He thinks toward us], *...thoughts of peace, and not of evil, to give* [us] *an expected end"* (Jeremiah 29:11). Knowing that God thinks this way toward us makes us a very special army--courageous yet compassionate conquerors. The scriptures call us, *"more than conquerors"* (Romans 8:37). Elijah exemplified the character of the Spirit-led conqueror in the denouement of 2 Kings 6.

When the king of Syria realized that it was the prophet Elisha who was revealing his battle plans to the king of Israel, he was determined to capture and kill Elijah. Only an uncircumcised, disconnected, sinner could deceive himself into believing that he can capture a man who had already proven that he could predict his every move. But Elisha wanted to be found.

The Syrians surrounded Elisha's camp, and in response to his worried servant's fears, Elisha made a declaration that comforts and encourages the armies of God to this day. *"Fear not: for they that be with us are more than they that be with them"* (2 Kings 6:16).

There were thousands of trained Soldiers surrounding Elijah's camp. But he was unafraid. The prophet knew what to do. First of all, *"Elisha prayed, and said, LORD, I pray thee, open his [his servant's] eyes, that he may see. And the LORD opened the eyes of the young man; and he saw: and, behold, the mountain was full of horses and chariots of fire round about Elisha"* (2 Kings 6:17). Elisha knew that he had unseen help. If you will listen to the prophets, you will know that too.

What happened next can only happen when you know that you are more than a conqueror.

> *"And when they came down to him, Elisha prayed unto the LORD, and said, Smite this people, I pray thee, with blindness. And he smote them with blindness according to the word of Elisha.*
>
> *And Elisha said unto them, This is not the way, neither is this the city: follow me, and I will bring you to the man whom ye seek. But he led them to Samaria.*
>
> *And it came to pass, when they were come into Samaria, that Elisha said, LORD, open the eyes of these men, that they may see. And the LORD opened their eyes, and they saw; and, behold, they were in the midst of Samaria.*
>
> *And the king of Israel said unto Elisha, when he saw them, My father, shall I smite them? shall I smite them?*

And he answered, Thou shalt not smite them: would-est thou smite those whom thou hast taken captive with thy sword and with thy bow? set bread and water before them, that they may eat and drink, and go to their master" (2 Kings 6:18-22).

Imagine that. The enemy was defeated and disoriented. All that was left was to utterly destroy them. Instead, the prophet of God, speaking from the heart of God, instructed the king to give his enemy bread and water and send them safely home. Have we not been instructed to do the same? Didn't Jesus, the King of kings, say, *"Love your enemies, bless them that curse you, do good to them that hate you, and pray for them which despitefully use you, and persecute you; That ye may be the children of your Father which is in heaven: for he maketh his sun to rise on the evil and on the good, and sendeth rain on the just and on the unjust"* (Matthew 5:44-45)?

This fivefold ministry gift is essential for displacing the principalities on the economic mountain. The prophetic utterance is critical to the transfer of wealth that God has declared shall take place.

But as we are *gathering the spoils of war*, (2 Chronicles 20:20-25), *converting the abundance of the sea*, (Isaiah 60:5), and *eating the riches of the Gentiles*, (Isaiah 61:6), let us remember *what Spirit we are of.* (Luke 9:54-56) Let us not forget that *vengeance is the Lord's* (Hebrews 10:30) and *it is not for us to know the times or the seasons which the Father has put in His own power.* No, He *has given us power to be witnesses unto Him.* Yes, we are the army of God, but we have been *named the Priests of the LORD.* Men call us *the Ministers of our God.* (Isaiah 61:6)

God has indeed called us to prosper. But like Joseph the dreamer, our prosperity is not purely for our own benefit. We are called to use our gifts to deliver even our enemies from destruction. (Genesis 39:2)

We have found a hidden treasure that Jesus has bought and paid for with his blood. (Matthew 13:44) Having this world's good, how can we say we love God and shut up our bowels of compassion from a lost and dying world? (1 John 3:16-18) Truly, *the whole earth is full of God's glory.* (Isaiah 6:3) His glory is all of God's goodness. (Exodus 33:17-19). God's riches are in His glory. (Philippians 4:19) And God has promised that *the whole earth will be filled with the knowledge of his glory.* (Habbakuk 2:14) Some of us have found out that God's glory is more than a spiritual concept. God's glory has tangible value. Some of us know that *the silver is God's and the gold is God's.* (Haggai 2:6-9)

That is why believers must free themselves and others from the Babylonian world system. The princes of the power of the air and all their kingdoms will be shaken (Hebrews 12:25-29). But the prophet has declared that *"it shall come to pass in the last days, that the mountain of the LORD's house shall be established in the top of the mountains, and shall be exalted above the hills; and all nations shall flow unto it"* (Isaiah 2:2) Amen!

Chapter 14
Give Me
This Mountain

And he called his ten servants, and delivered them ten
pounds, and said unto them, Occupy till I come.

Luke 19:13

Before Moses died, he sent twelve spies into the Promised
Land to *"see the land, what it is, and the people that dwell-*
eth therein, whether they be strong or weak, few or many;
And what the land is that they dwell in, whether it be good
or bad; and what cities they be that they dwell in, whether
in tents, or in strong holds; And what the land is, whether it
be fat or lean, whether there be wood therein, or not." He
instructed the spies to be *"of good courage, and bring of the*
fruit of the land" (Numbers 13:18-20). In short, He wanted
them to gather information and bring back an encouraging
report to the children of Israel.

All of the spies came back having observed the very same
thing. They all said, *"We came unto the land whither thou*
sentest us, and surely it floweth with milk and honey; and
this is the fruit of it" (Numbers 13:18-27). They all agreed
that what God had told Moses about the land was, indeed,
true. But there was considerable disagreement about their
ability to possess what they had observed.

Ten of the twelve came back with, what the Bible calls, an evil report. They were terrified of the obstacles (specifically the giants) that stood between them and what God said was theirs and their fears struck terror in the hearts of all who heard their assessment of the situation.

Even though they agreed that what Moses said about the land was true, they held that truth in fearful unrighteousness and declared, *"the people be strong that dwell in the land, and the cities are walled, and very great: and moreover we saw the children of Anak there.*

The Amalekites dwell in the land of the south: and the Hittites, and the Jebusites, and the Amorites, dwell in the mountains: and the Canaanites dwell by the sea, and by the coast of Jordan" (Numbers 13:28-29).

One of the spies, Caleb, tried to avert their fears, much like Jesus who said to Jairus upon hearing that his daughter was dead, *"Be not afraid, only believe"* (Mark 5:36). Caleb said, *"Let us go up at once, and possess it; for we are well able to overcome it."* But the Bible says, *"the men that went up with him said, We be not able to go up against the people; for they are stronger than we.*

And they brought up an evil report of the land which they had searched unto the children of Israel, saying, The land, through which we have gone to search it, is a land that eateth up the inhabitants thereof; and all the people that we saw in it are men of a great stature. And there we saw the giants, the sons of Anak, which come of the giants: and we were in our own sight as grasshoppers, and so we were in their sight" (Numbers 13:28-29).

98

Can you imagine being that close to the realization of your dream only to be discouraged by the fears of people who won't trust God? The generation of people that listened to that evil report died in the wilderness. They never set foot in the Promised Land. And, what's worse, their unbelief caused their children to have to wait almost forty years to enjoy what was already theirs for the taking. But don't forget: there were two spies who brought back a good report.

Caleb said and Joshua agreed, *"Let us go up at once, and possess it; for we are well able to overcome it."* So when Moses died, Joshua became the leader of the children of Israel. Joshua led the children of those who believed not across Jordan into the Promised Land and Caleb was right by his side. Surely Joshua was so preoccupied with his new leadership responsibilities that he didn't have time to dwell on past failures. But Caleb never forgot the victory he was denied by the unbelieving spies.

When *"the children of Judah came unto Joshua in Gilgal:"* the Bible says, *"Caleb the son of Jephunneh the Kenezite said unto* [Joshua], *Thou knowest the thing that the LORD said unto Moses the man of God concerning me and thee in Kadeshbarnea.*

Forty years old was I when Moses the servant of the LORD sent me from Kadeshbarnea to espy out the land; and I brought him word again as it was in mine heart. Nevertheless my brethren that went up with me made the heart of the people melt: but I wholly followed the LORD my God. And Moses sware on that day, saying, Surely the land whereon thy feet have trodden shall be thine inheritance, and thy children's for ever, because thou hast wholly followed the LORD my God.

And now, behold, the LORD hath kept me alive, as he said, these forty and five years, even since the LORD spake this word unto Moses, while the children of Israel wandered in the wilderness: and now, lo, I am this day fourscore and five years old.

As yet I am as strong this day as I was in the day that Moses sent me: as my strength was then, even so is my strength now, for war, both to go out, and to come in.

Now therefore give me this mountain, whereof the LORD spake in that day; for thou heardest in that day how the Ana-kims were there, and that the cities were great and fenced: if so be the LORD will be with me, then I shall be able to drive them out, as the LORD said" (Joshua 14:6-12).

Caleb had been waiting and dreaming for forty years. He didn't sit idly by and hope something good would happen. No, he stayed in shape. He formulated plans. He encouraged himself in the Lord his God. Caleb knew that *"a dream cometh through the multitude of business,"* (Ecclesiastes 5:3) so he kept himself busy until it was time to realize his dream.

The Bible says, *"Joshua blessed [Caleb], and gave unto Ca-leb the son of Jephunneh Hebron for an inheritance. Hebron therefore became the inheritance of Caleb the son of Jep-hunneh the Kenezite unto this day, because that he wholly followed the LORD God of Israel. And the name of Hebron before was Kirjatharba; which Arba was a great man among the Anakims. And the land had rest from war"* (Joshua 14:13-15).

And the land had rest from war.

Looking at the world we live in can be terribly discouraging. Is there no rest for the weary? People don't seem at all interested in the things of God. And, far too often, like the ten spies with the evil report, the church seems so terrified of the people she is called to evangelize that her prevailing message is one of "escape" rather than "occupy." We seem to be reliving the travails of Hosea.

> *"Hear the word of the LORD, ye children of Israel: for the LORD hath a controversy with the inhabitants of the land, because there is no truth, nor mercy, nor knowledge of God in the land. By swearing, and lying, and killing, and stealing, and committing adultery, they break out, and blood toucheth blood.*
>
> *Therefore shall the land mourn, and every one that dwelleth therein shall languish, with the beasts of the field, and with the fowls of heaven; yea, the fishes of the sea also shall be taken away.*
>
> *Yet let no man strive, nor reprove another: for thy people are as they that strive with the priest. Therefore shalt thou fall in the day, and the prophet also shall fall with thee in the night, and I will destroy thy mother.*
>
> *My people are destroyed for lack of knowledge: because thou hast rejected knowledge, I will also reject thee, that thou shalt be no priest to me: seeing thou hast forgotten the law of thy God, I will also forget thy children"* (Hosea 4:1-6).

Our nation is sanctioning the senseless murder of millions of babies, through legalized abortion, every year. Wise fools are daily descending to the degrading depths of sodomy and bestiality and desperately trying to demand the 'right' to live wrong. We incarcerate more of our citizens than any other nation on the planet. Our educational system is failing miserably; dropout rates are rising and discipline has all but disappeared. And our national debt appears to be an unstoppable juggernaut. The natural man might call our situation hopeless. But we are led by the Spirit. Yes, Jesus is coming to get us and we lovingly await his appearing. But he told us to *"occupy"* until he comes. (See Luke 19:13)

The word 'occupy' is a military term, and is means to secure, hold and then to advance. If there were a strategic territory in which the enemy was occupying, then the Army would be given orders, to displace the enemy by securing it, holding it and then moving out to take other territory until victory is won.

Conversely, Jesus, our commander-in-chief, has given us orders to displace the demonic forces atop of each of these mountains, by securing the strongholds, holding our ground by not giving place to the Devil, and then moving forward. This tactic is what I am calling, 'Advancing the Kingdom of God'.

Lieutenant Colonel Gerald Sharpless (US Army Retired) told me, "War has always been about taking (occupying) ground." As Soldiers, we were well trained to either secure key terrain needed for a mission or circumvent secondary obstructions that were between our objective and us. Soldiers know how to take the high ground. The same principles apply in the Army of God.

Remember how we redefined the word re•pent by breaking it into two syllables; 'Re' meaning to do over or go back to, and 'pent' speaking of things that are higher as in penthouse? Repent, then, could mean to return to a higher place--our highest place. The Kingdom of God represents the place we held before the fall of Adam and we are well able to retake this mountain. Let me show you how.

Sharpless says, "in order to take a hill or a mountain--the high ground--if you will, you need a few basic things: an avenue of approach, cover and concealment, a means of communication, the ability to identify your position, air support or long range fire, ground support or suppressive fire, and the courage to close in on and ultimately destroy the enemy or enemies that occupy your objective."

For ages, this approach has gone unchanged and the spiritual parallels are incredible.

Our avenue of approach to all things is faith. *"Through faith we understand that the worlds were framed by the word of God, so that things which are seen were not made of things which do appear"* (Hebrews 11:3). God regained the earth, the earth that Satan destroyed when he fell, through faith. We will reclaim the earth that sin and sinners are currently occupying and destroying through faith.

Grace through faith will save sinners (Ephesians 2:8-10). Saints will please God through faith (Hebrews 11:6). Our ɛ ɪemies will be made to be at peace with us and *"the land* [will have] *rest from war"* because we have pleased God through faith (Joshua 14:15 / Proverbs 16:7). We live by faith (Habakkuk 2:4 / Romans 1:16,17). And unlike the spies who brought back the evil report because they were afraid of what they had seen, *"we walk by faith, not by sight"* (2 Corinthians 5:7). Our approach, like our God, remains unchanged. We will take the high ground by faith.

The blood of the Lamb and the word of our testimony cover, protect, us from things that might kill us. (Revelation 12:10-12) We are also concealed (hidden from plain sight--especially from the air) by the armor and righteousness of God. (Ephesians 6:10-17) Our lives are literally *"hid with Christ in God"* (Colossians 3:3).

Prior to engaging our enemies in close quarter combat, we can call for the air support or long-range missile fire of prayer. GPS (God's Positioning System) assures us that our Heavenly Father knows exactly where we are at all times. Not one sparrow falls to the ground without His knowledge and He has assured us that *"we are of more value than many sparrows"* (Matthew 10:31 / Luke 12:7). While others are fearfully calling out coordinates, we can obey our God and fear not, because, not only does he know exactly where we are, but Jehovah Nissi--*The Lord Our Banner*--has the very hairs of our heads numbered. Truly, His banner over us is love.

When we pray, we can count on the angels of heaven to bombard our enemies on land, air, and sea, just like Michael the archangel wrestled with the prince of Persia on Daniel's behalf.

And as we prepare to approach the enemy, we can call for the supportive, suppressive fire of praise and worship to confuse and distract the enemy. With our hands lifted up and our feet on the ground, our hearts filled with praise and our mouths filled with worship, we can make sure the enemy keeps his unholy head down, not knowing what is hitting him or where it is coming from until it is way too late.

All of this, however, will be of little consequence if we are not willing to courageously engage those who possess our possessions, prepared to violently take what is ours by force. Jesus said, *"from the days of John the Baptist until now the kingdom of heaven suffereth violence, and the violent take it by force"* (Matthew 11:12).

Michael E. Evans, whom I quoted earlier, has been sharing a revelation with us concerning the unreaped harvests that await the body of Christ. According to Evans, we have sown much, but through a misguided doctrine of delay and escape, many of us have found reason after reason to talk about some future victory, some potential harvest, and some coming revival. But Evans says, Jesus is saying, *"Lift up your eyes, and look on the fields; for they are white already to harvest"* (John 4:35). That message demands immediate action from the body of Christ.

Paul warned us to, *"Be not deceived; God is not mocked: for whatsoever a man soweth, that shall he also reap. For he that soweth to his flesh shall of the flesh reap corruption; but he that soweth to the Spirit shall of the Spirit reap life everlasting"* (Galatians 6:7-8).

Paul went on to encourage us to *"not be weary in well doing: for in due season"* He promised, *"we shall reap, if we faint not."* Sadly, according to Evans, Christians are incredibly weary and fainting daily precisely because they have not reaped. Well that day is over.

We are well able to take this mountain!

We will see revival in our lifetime. We will walk in divine health, live to a ripe old age, full of years, and leave an inheritance to our children's children. While we are here, we will build goodly houses, establish powerful churches, write great books, sing glorious songs, develop witty inventions, start successful businesses, bless--even lend to--nations, and prepare ourselves so that our soon-and-coming King will, indeed, *find faith on the earth when he returns.* (See Luke 18:8:)

Our approach is faith and faith is always NOW!

Our cover and concealment is the blood of the Lamb, the word of our testimony, and the armor and righteousness of God.

Our air support is the power of prayer.

Our supportive suppressive fire comes through praise and worship.

And we are not afraid to engage the enemy.

"In all things we are more than conquerors through him that loved us" (Romans 8:37). *"Greater is he that is in us than he that is in the world"* (1 John 4:4). *"Our God always leadeth us in triumph in Christ"* (2 Corinthians 2:14). And *"God has not given us the spirit of fear; but of power, and of love, and of a sound mind"* (2 Timothy 1:7).

We declare and decree: Give us this mountain!

 106

The Beloved Community

Chapter 15

I Have A Dream

We've got some difficult days ahead. But it doesn't matter with me now. Because I've been to the mountaintop. And I don't mind. Like anybody, I would like to live a long life. Longevity has its place. But I'm not concerned about that now. I just want to do God's will. And He's allowed me to go up to the mountain. And I've looked over. And I've seen the Promised land. I may not get there with you. But I want you to know tonight, that we, as a people, will get to the Promised land. So I'm happy, tonight. I'm not worried about anything. I'm not fearing any man. Mine eyes have seen the glory of the coming of the Lord.

Martin Luther King, Jr.
April 3, 1968
Mason Temple
(Church of God in Christ Headquarters)
Memphis, Tennessee

Most people know that Dr. Martin Luther King, Jr. had A Dream. Some people know the Bible says, *"a dream cometh through the multitude of business; and a fool's voice is known by multitude of words."* (Ecclesiastes 5:3) But how many people know that Dr. Martin Luther King, Jr. also had a plan to realize his dream? That plan meant work--*a multitude of business*, if you will--for the self-proclaimed followers of his dream.

Keep the dream alive? I think Dr. King might much prefer that we wake up, shut up, get up, and gear up to put his plan to realize his dream to work. But never mind what I think. In an address to the N.A.A.C.P. in December of 1956 called *Facing The Challenge Of A New Age*, Dr. King said it best.

"We have before us the glorious opportunity to inject a new dimension of love into the veins of our civilization. There is still a voice crying out in terms that echo across the generations, saying; 'Love your enemies, bless them that curse you, pray for them that despitefully use you, that you may be the children of your Father which is in Heaven.'" "The end," He contended, "is reconciliation, the end is redemption, the end is the creation of the community."

The creation of the community is a joint-venture with God; it is working to make real in our life-time the Biblical model of community or the 'beloved community'.

So, what is this 'Beloved Community'?

Well, first of all, it must be noted that the beloved community, like Dr. King, has its origin, its roots, if you will, in the New Testament and the church that it birthed. Jesus, while here on earth, was the personification of the beloved community. He was God manifest in the flesh. And I believe the mission of the church is to manifest that beloved community, as well.

All the synoptic gospel writers mention the term 'beloved' in their writings. Matthew, for example, wrote, *"And lo a voice from heaven, saying, This is my beloved Son, in whom*

I am well pleased" (Matthew 3:17). Mark recounted Jesus' parable of the frustrated owner of a vineyard, *"Having yet therefore one son, his well beloved, he sent him also last unto them, saying, They will reverence my son"* (Mark 12:6). And like Matthew, Luke references the baptism of Jesus and notes the voice of God saying, *"This is my beloved Son"* (Luke 3:22).

God, the creator of the universe, uses the word *'beloved'* to describe His son. And John 3:16, says that *"God so loved the world, that he gave his only begotten Son* [His beloved], *that whosoever believeth in him should not perish, but have everlasting life."* 1 John 3:16 clarifies that, *"Hereby perceive we the love of God, because he laid down his life for us."* That passage of scripture further suggests that we, in light of the Father's great act of love, *"ought to lay down our lives for the brethren."*

Those ideas let us know, not only, the depth of God's love for us, but the height of His expectation of us. God wants to see His love manifest through us toward a lost and dying world. That is the foundation of the beloved community. God proclaimed through the prophet Jeremiah, *"I know the thoughts that I think toward you, saith the LORD, thoughts of peace, and not of evil, to give you an expected end"* (Jeremiah 29:11).

God sowed Jesus as a seed and in so doing, fulfilled Jesus' mandate in John 12:24 and brought forth the fruit of the church. Now the church must fulfill its ordained commission to bring forth much fruit, fruit that remains, the fruit of the beloved community.

I believe God wants us to "end" up as His 'beloved' through faith in His beloved son. I also believe He expects that faith, displayed through our works (*"Faith without works is dead"* (James 2:20).), to help this world, His world, become the beloved community. Dr. King's writings make it clear that he wanted the concept of brotherhood to "become a reality." And he believed that our loyalties had to "transcend our race, our tribe, our class, and our nation."

Now some might say that Dr. King and subsequent advocates of the beloved community are endeavoring to regulate righteousness or politicize piety. It has been argued that brotherhood is not something that can be enforced by law. And there is a degree of validity to such arguments. But laws are not designed to change hearts. Laws and the agencies that enforce them are designed to govern behavior. You don't have to like me or even believe that I am a human being, but righteous laws rigorously enforced by right thinking men, will ensure that you will treat me like a man or suffer serious consequences.

Dr. King was an American citizen. His faith was in Jesus and his dream was born of God's Spirit, but he was also aware of his Constitutional rights. Having displayed his Constitutional cognizance in his *I Have A Dream* speech, it is not unreasonable to assume that he might also point detractors of the beloved community to the US Constitution, which begins with these words:

We the people of the United States, in order to form a more perfect union, establish Justice, insure domestic tranquility, provide for the common defense, promote the general welfare, and secure the blessings of liberty to ourselves and our posterity, do ordain and establish this Constitution for the United States of America.

Embodied in this defining document are all the elements of the beloved community. And there to undergird this defining document are the foundational peaks of the seven mountains we have described. Is it possible the framers of the US Constitution were seeking a type of beloved community of their own? They were, after all, seeking "a more perfect union."

The words 'union' and 'community' come from similar roots. Union, from the Latin *unio* or *unus*, meaning one or oneness is, in fact, a sub set of community, or common unity, from the Latin *comm-unis*, or shared oneness. Even our unofficial national motto, *E Pluribus Unum*, meaning one from many, speaks of the desire to create and live in a society where people from differing backgrounds labor to live together.

The power that the people give their representatives and officers to govern behavior is necessary in order to maintain a harmonious balance between differing elements. Such a society must find a way, then, to establish justice.

Justice has always been a function of earthly wisdom guided by heavenly truth. The fact that the founding fathers agreed is evidenced in the very first entry to the US Bill of Rights.

> "Congress shall make no law respecting an establishment of religion, or prohibiting the free exercise thereof."

113

If people are to live in a just society, they need the freedom to commune with a just God without the interference of unjust men. Hence the official motto of the US, adopted in 1956, *In God We Trust.* Religion, then, must be unfettered if the beloved community is to thrive. Equally as important, education must be available to all and that availability is heavily dependent upon a thriving economy. Actually the economy and the education system are interdependent.

Domestic tranquility has always been secured through a community commitment to honor the rights of others and/or the authority of those who protect the rights of others. The common defense is provided for by the common economy and the common economy is created by the general welfare.

At the end of the day, then, the beloved community will be established by "We the people." We, the people, will secure and celebrate the blessings of liberty for our families and the generations that follow us by establishing laws that demand behavior that is a reflection of our highest ideals.

The apostles and the prophets spoke of the beloved community.

> *"And it shall come to pass in that day, I will hear, saith the LORD, I will hear the heavens, and they shall hear the earth; And the earth shall hear the corn, and the wine, and the oil; and they shall hear Jezreel." Hosea 2:21-23*

> *"And I will sow her unto me in the earth; and I will have mercy upon her that had not obtained mercy; and I will say to them which were not my people, Thou*

114

art my people; and they shall say, Thou art my God.

As he saith also in Osee, I will call them my people, which were not my people; and her beloved, which was not beloved." Romans 9:25
"But ye are a chosen generation, a royal priesthood, an holy nation, a peculiar people; that ye should shew forth the praises of him who hath called you out of darkness into his marvellous light;

Which in time past were not a people, but are now the people of God: which had not obtained mercy, but now have obtained mercy." 1 Peter 2:9-10

The church (the true beloved community) is the mystery spoken of by the Apostle Paul…

"And he said unto them, Unto you it is given to know the mystery of the kingdom of God: but unto them that are without, all these things are done in parables:" Mark 4:11

"This is a great mystery: but I speak concerning Christ and the church." Ephesians 5:32

We find the code of conduct for the beloved community in 3 John 4-11.

"I have no greater joy than to hear that my children walk in truth.

Beloved, thou doest faithfully whatsoever thou doest to the brethren, and to strangers; Which have borne

witness of thy charity before the church: whom if thou bring forward on their journey after a godly sort, thou shalt do well: Because that for his name's sake they went forth, taking nothing of the Gentiles.

We therefore ought to receive such, that we might be fellowhelpers to the truth.

I wrote unto the church: but Diotrephes, who loveth to have the preeminence among them, receiveth us not.

Wherefore, if I come, I will remember his deeds which he doeth, prating against us with malicious words: and not content therewith, neither doth he himself receive the brethren, and forbiddeth them that would, and casteth them out of the church.

Beloved, follow not that which is evil, but that which is good. He that doeth good is of God: but he that doeth evil hath not seen God."

And we find the beloved community consummated in the city of Jerusalem, Revelation 20:9.

"And they went up on the breadth of the earth, and compassed the camp of the saints about, and the beloved city."

Dr. Martin Luther King, Jr.'s dream was a vision of a completely integrated society, a community of love and justice wherein brotherhood would be an actuality in all of social life. In his mind, such a community would be the ideal corporate expression of the Christian faith.

Dr. King believed that it was God's intention that everyone should have the physical and spiritual necessities of life. He could not envision the Beloved Community apart from the alleviation of economic inequity and the achievement of economic justice.

Martin Luther King, Jr. was a twentieth century prophet, just like Amos was an eighth century prophet. Amos declared the word of the Lord to his generation, *" Let justice roll down like water, and righteousness like a mighty stream. "*

While much has occurred to rid America of legalized segregation, we have yet to realize true integration. Integration will occur in the hearts of men and women who see themselves as interrelated and interdependent upon one another, and are connected by choice in authentic relationships for the purpose of realizing their God-given destinies.

For this cause, we are mobilizing an Army of God to advance His kingdom in the earth realm. As born-again believers, we are liberated by Jesus Christ from all evil including racism. We are empowered by the Holy spirit to live a transforming personal life, networking to make the church the body of Christ where all of God's children worship together in all spheres (mountains) of society. We are making the 'Beloved Community' a reality in our generation.

Just as Martin Luther King, Jr. served his generation as a prophetic voice in the twentieth century, there is a need for prophets to be raised up in the twenty-first century. Prophets who will speak to, not only to the church or religious mountain, but to each of the seven mountains in every culture in order to bring about genuine transformation for generations yet unborn.

I like what the Bible says about King David. *"David, after he had served his own generation by the will of God, fell asleep, was buried with his fathers, and saw corruption."* It was only after David had served his generation and fulfilled his destiny, that he fell asleep. Our generation needs to hear and see the gospel of the kingdom and I believe that it is our time to rise and shine, so that the glory of the Lord will be displayed.

Chapter 16
Faith - The Currency of The Kingdom

Now faith is the substance of things hoped for,
the evidence of things not seen.

Hebrews 11:1

If we are to serve our generation and fulfill our destiny, we are going to need more than a dream. Remember: *"a dream cometh through the multitude of business; and a fool's voice is known by multitude of words"* (Ecclesiastes 5:3). If we are going to be about the business of the kingdom, we are going to have to walk by faith. When it comes to realizing dreams, faith is the coin of the realm. Faith is the currency of the kingdom.

Faith is the substance of things hoped for and we are hoping to see the beloved community become a reality in our world. Hope is focused on the future. We don't see the beloved community yet. If we did see it we would have no need for hope. Hope focuses on the future, but faith, the substance of things hoped for, transcends time and space.

Faith is now. Like God, who always IS, faith is eternal, ever present, unchanging.

As the Army of God we must always remember that the battle is not ours, but the Lord's. The only fight that we are told to fight is the good fight of faith. It is a good fight because we always win when we walk by faith. It is our faith that will empower us to be victorious as we ascend to the top of our mountain.

HOW TO FIGHT THE 'GOOD FIGHT' OF FAITH

Fight the good fight of faith, lay hold on eternal life,
to which you were also called and have confessed the good
confession in the presence of many witnesses.

I Timothy 6:12

In order to successfully fight the good fight of faith, we must first have a working definition of faith. Based on Hebrews Chapter 11 and verse 1, one definition for faith is this: Faith is an action, based on a belief system, sustained by confidence, over a period of time.

You see our belief system is what determines our ability to fight our enemy, Satan and his host of angels or demons. As believers, if our belief system is based on the world's ideas and human reasoning, we will find ourselves trying to fight demonic forces on their ground. Let me tell you that will be a bad fight, because we will lose every time. On the other hand, if our belief system is based on God's Word, we'll be able to fight the good fight, which means we win every time.

120

In order to become effective 'mountain climbers' we must change our belief system to agree with the Word of God, which is a fight in and of it self because it runs counter to our natural way of thinking. This is the renewing your mind, which the Apostle Paul speaks about in Romans 12:1-2. Make a bold decision now to become a faithful disciple for Jesus Christ, by becoming a faithful follower. Jesus said, *" If anyone would follow me, let him deny himself, and take up his cross daily, and follow me"* (Luke 9:23).

As we wage the good fight, as the Army of God, it is important to understand that there is a military strategy of fighting on four battle fronts.

The first front that we must fight on is our hearing. *"So then faith comes by hearing and hearing by the word of God"* (Romans 10:17). In other words, you believe what you continually hear. So we must sanctify or separate ourselves from ungodly influences and negative, unbelieving people. This means cutting ties with some so called friends, parting ways with people whose agenda is different from yours. In a practical way, it means to stop listening to certain radio stations, DVD's and CD's. It means to stop watching certain movies that violate the principles of God's Word. In the work place, it means to stop taking your lunch break in certain areas where gossip and filthy conversations are the order of the day.

In a word, you'll have to fight to make sure you are hearing the things that align with Kingdom living. Because what you allow to enter your ear gates will shape your belief system. And your belief system will dictate your actions, and your actions will demonstrate the level of your faith.

The second front on which we must engage the enemy is the battlefield of your mind. The Apostle Paul writes in 2 Corinthians 10:3-5, *"For though we walk in the flesh, we do not war after the flesh: (For the weapons of our warfare are not carnal, but mighty through God to the pulling down of strong holds;) Casting down imaginations, and every high thing that exalteth itself against the knowledge of God, and bringing into captivity every thought to the obedience of Christ."*

The only power that Satan has over a believer is in the mind, the power of suggestive thoughts. Now, if the truth is told, all of us have thoughts that could be considered evil at times. Satan and his demonic forces will make sure you are bombarded with some very tempting thoughts. But having the thoughts or being tempted is not the problem and we should not feel guilty because of them. We get into trouble when we entertain such thoughts--think about them over and over, meditate on them.

Take authority over those wrong thoughts in Jesus' name. Bring them into captivity by speaking the word and the promises of God to Satan--out loud . You see, as long as you just think about it, you are only making it a mental battle. You are only fighting on Satan's terrain. You will lose every time. However, when you start confessing the Word, praying in the Spirit, decreeing that the blood of Jesus covers your mind, you make Satan fight on your terrain.

Speak to Satan. Say something like this. "Devil you are a liar and you have been defeated; you have no place in my thought life, in the name of Jesus!" Then talk to yourself, and tell yourself, "Self, you are redeemed from every curse of the law, and you are the righteousness of God in Christ Jesus!"

Sure, it will be a fight for you to do that. People might think you are crazy, and Satan will try to convince you that it is no harm to think certain thoughts because no one will ever know what you are thinking. But the Devil is a liar, and Jesus is the Messiah! You cannot afford the luxury of remaining silent. Your very life is at stake. Your witness as a follower of Jesus Christ is the crux of the whole matter. So, cast down every thought that does not line up with God's Word.

The third front on which we must engage the enemy is revealed in Romans 10:8. *"But what saith it? The word is nigh thee, even in thy mouth, and in thy heart: that is, the word of faith, which we preach."* To enforce your victory over Satan, the Word of God must not only be in your heart, it must be in your mouth. If you tend to be one of those persons who just says whatever comes up, this may be one of your toughest battles. Your flesh will pressure you to talk about the problem instead of God's promises. Your flesh will drive you to speak symptoms and get sympathy instead of speaking the Word and declaring your victory. But don't give in to your flesh.

Several years ago, my wife and I believed God to be debt-free. There were days when thoughts would emerge like; "This stuff of believing and confessing really doesn't work!" or "It is foolish to pile your bills up and speak to them or to stand on them in as a gesture of taking authority over them."

I must admit some days the demonic forces won the battle in my mind and I did not make my confessions of faith. But then I would repent and ask God to forgive me and I'd get right back in the fight with more vigor. Now, we are debt free. Glory to God!

Fight the good fight of faith. Walk in the power of the Spirit. And be an overcomer in Jesus' name! Then you are ready to fight on the fourth front in this 'good fight of faith'.

The fourth front may be the toughest one of all--the battle-field of action. James 2:17 says, *"Even so faith, if it hath not works, is dead, being alone."* So begin to act on what you believe.

Walk in love toward those who have mistreated you, lied on you and stabbed you in your back. Resist those fleshly impulses that make you want to give them their just due. Obey the word and bless those that curse you. Even when finances were tight, my wife and I kept tithing. We kept sowing into other ministries, and we kept looking for opportunities to be a blessing to other people. What were we doing? We were being *"doers of the word, and not hearers only"* (James 1:22). We were working the Word, knowing that the Word works if you work it.

Fight the good fight of faith by keeping the Word in your ears, taking your thoughts captive, speaking and acting on the Word of God. Maintain that tenacity, that pit-bull like mindset that refuses to quit or give up. Fight on all four fronts and you will win every time in Jesus' name.

It was by faith that sister Cleo Greenhill prepared punch and cookies and a Bible lesson for Detroit's inner-city children. By faith I came back and kept coming back to church.

I fought the good fight of faith, went to church in Sacramento, and met Cinda Finch. By faith I found my good thing and I continue to walk in the favor of God. I bought that '62 Oldsmobile by faith. It was my very first car. Every man buys his first car by faith. And faith got us through the trauma of that terrible accident.

By faith, I asked Cinda Finch to marry me. By faith she said yes. By faith we went to Japan as one.

By faith we were connected with the McMillans who had also obtained *"like precious faith"* (2 Peter 1:1). By faith we started the Yokota Angelic Gospel Choir and were a blessing to the men and women in uniform.

My faith forced me past my fears and false perceptions to hear what a white chaplain could possibly say about a black leader. God used this chaplain to inspire me to the chaplaincy. God used this chaplain to break down the middle wall of partition--the wall of racism. My heavenly Father also used this chaplain to disciple me. I fought the good fight of faith and began to walk out my destiny.

Behold, his soul which is lifted up is not upright in him: but the just shall live by his faith. Habakkuk 2:4

For therein is the righteousness of God revealed from faith to faith: as it is written, The just shall live by faith. Romans 1:17

(For we walk by faith, not by sight:) 2 Corinthians 5:7

But without faith it is impossible to please him: for he that cometh to God must believe that he is, and that he is a rewarder of them that diligently seek him. Hebrews 11:6

I live by faith. If you are not born again by the Spirit of the living God, having had your sins washed clean by the shed blood of the risen Lamb of Glory, Jesus Christ, you are dead in trespasses and sins and will not enter into eternal life. If you want life, and that more abundantly, you must receive it by faith.

I walk by faith. I have seen too much, on and off the battle-field, to know that I can't trust my eyes. I know that *"Eye hath not seen, nor ear heard, neither have entered into the heart of man, the things which God hath prepared for them that love him. But God hath revealed them unto us by his Spirit: for the Spirit searcheth all things, yea, the deep things of God"* (1 Corinthians 2:9-10). If you want to see all that God has prepared for you, you must look through the eyes of faith.

I want to please God. And I know that if I have any hope of pleasing God, I'm going to have to do so by faith. I know that *"When a man's ways please the LORD, he maketh even his enemies to be at peace with him"* (Proverbs 16:7). I had very real enemies in the military and I have very real enemies in The Army of God. I need to please God so I can walk in peace. You do too.

My faith journey took me to Fresno, California, to pastor The Church of the Living God (C.W.F.F.) Temple #12, and brought me to the Department of Veterans Affairs. By faith I was connected with Chaplain Donald Welsh who introduced me to the Army Reserves.

Faith found a way around the ecclesiastical mountain that had interrupted my dream. Faith fulfilled my dream of becoming a military chaplain.

Surely St. Martin of Tours was walking by faith when he cut his cloak in half and clothed the naked beggar. Surely he knew that *"Faith without works is dead"* and that he could not simply say to that man *"be thou warmed and filled."* Surely faith made him willing to go to the front lines of a battlefield, unarmed, to prove that he was not a coward. Surely faith foresaw his future, and mine, and ended that battled to spare his life?

Faith fuels the courage of US Soldiers everyday as they risk life and limb to protect the freedoms of family, friends, and even discouraging detractors.

Faith and faith alone brought me through twenty-nine years of military service. Faith in a faithful God and the faithfulness of a faithful wife and family carried me through the oppressive darkness I experienced in the Middle East. Faith in a faithful God and the faithfulness of a faithful wife and family encouraged me to stage revivals in the desert. Faith in a faithful God and the faithfulness of a faithful wife and family were the foundation upon which men and women were saved and healed and filled with the Holy Ghost. Faith in a faithful God and the faithfulness of a faithful wife and family protected me daily and brought me home safely.

As I end this book and begin the next chapter of my life, I know that faith will stand under my hope of seeing, even helping to establish, the beloved community in the earth.

By faith Cinda and I are laboring daily to mobilize The Army of God to fight the good fight of faith. Our generation needs to hear and see the gospel of the kingdom and I believe that it is our time to rise and shine, so that the glory of the Lord will be displayed.

By faith, I am determined to one day say, *"I have fought a good fight, I have finished my course, I have kept the faith: Henceforth there is laid up for me a crown of righteousness, which the Lord, the righteous judge, shall give me at that day: and not to me only, but unto all them also that love his appearing"* (2 Timothy 4:7,8).

About The Herrings

Dr. Milton Herring is a graduate of Morehouse College and holds a BA in Business Administration. He also has a Masters of Divinity degree from Interdenominational Theological Center in Atlanta, Georgia and a Doctorate of Ministry degree from Southern California School of Ministry in Inglewood, California. Having pastored for many years, he is the founding pastor of Living Word Christian Church International located in Torrance, California and Living Word Christian Church in Kuwait.

Dr. Herring is a Vietnam era veteran and is a recently retired chaplain. He served as a Lieutenant Colonel in the United States Army Reserves. He was deployed in support of Iraqi Freedom serving in Kuwait (2004-05) and again deployed to Kuwait (2008-2009). He was pastor over the Gospel Services and was used by God to bring hundreds into the Kingdom of God and held the first revivals in Kuwait and Iraq for the military.

Pastor Cinda Herring serves as the senior pastor. Pastor Cinda has served the City of Torrance, California as a Civil Service Commissioner, Chairman of the Community Advisory Council for Family Preservation and South Bay Chapter President for the Network of Evangelical Women in Ministry. She also holds a bachelor of Arts degree in Business Administration and a Master of Arts degree in Organizational Management.

Pastors Milton and Cinda Herring were ordained by Bishop Keith A. Butler of Word of Faith International Christian Center headquartered in Southfield, Michigan. They have been married for 39 years and they have three sons and daughter-in-laws: Milton Jr., and Sherry, Mahlek (Maurice) and Ingrid, and Marcus and Niema. Their children have blessed them with ten grandchildren.

Bishop Milton & Pastor Cinda have a mandate to minister to churches around the world about how to implement kingdom principles in their cities. If you have been blessed by reading *Mobilizing the Army of God*, you will surely be blessed by the teaching and preaching ministry of Bishop Milton & Pastor Cinda Herring.

Availability:
Worldwide by arrangement

Contact:
Living Word Christian Church
P. O. Box 357
Torrance, Ca. 90508
(866) 280-5241
E-Mail: atkogmin@gmail.com